RECIPES FROM MEXICO CITY'S
STREETS, MARKETS & FONDAS

LESLEY TÉLLEZ

PHOTOGRAPHS BY
PENNY DE LOS SANTOS

KYLE BOOKS

For my parents and grandparents

Published in 2015 by Kyle Books
www.kylebooks.com
general.enquiries@kylebooks.com

Distributed by National Book Network
4501 Forbes Blvd., Suite 200
Lanham, MD 20706
Phone: (800) 462-6420
Fax: (800) 338-4550
customercare@nbnbooks.com

10 9 8 7 6 5 4 3 2 1

ISBN 978-1-909487-27-7

Text © 2015 by Lesley Téllez
Photography © 2015 by Penny De Los Santos
Book design © 2015 by Kyle Books Ltd

Designer: Little Mule Studio
Project editor: Anja Schmidt
Photographer: Penny De Los Santos
Food styling: Adrienne Anderson
Prop styling: Marina Malchin
Copy editor: Sarah Scheffel
Production: Nic Jones, Gemma John, and Lisa Pinnell

Library of Congress Control No. 2014960085

Color reproduction by ALTA London
Printed and bound in China by C&C Offset Printing Co., Ltd.

TABLE OF CONTENTS

SIEMPRE "CON TODO"

The first thing that struck me when I moved to Mexico City in 2009 was that I didn't recognize any of the food. I grew up in Southern California, one of the North American epicenters of Mexican food. But these Mexico City tacos—the ones that abounded on street corners, and in markets, and in *taquerías* whose lights stayed on until well past two a.m.—these tacos were gorgeous and wild and raw, like some species of animal long extinct.

At the slow-cooked beef *suadero* stands, a *taquero*, or taco maker, would lift a hunk of meat out of a caramel-colored moat of fat, revealing beef transformed into a glistening, crispy-edged confit. He'd chop it to bits with a large cleaver—*whack! whack! whack!*—and slap a tortilla on the grill, drizzling on a little extra fat like a kiss good-bye. "Con todo?" he'd ask. *With everything?* I learned to say yes. (For the love of God, yes. Always *con todo*.) He'd sprinkle on raw onion and fresh cilantro and place the taco on a plastic plate lined with a square of gray paper. Other hunks of meat remained bubbling in the fatty moat.

On almost every other street corner, a *trompo*, or roasting spit, lay stacked with orangey red marinated pork, cooked until juicy and blackened in spots. Men in aprons and triangular hats worked fast, slicing meat off the cylinder of pork and catching it in cupped hands lined with tortillas. "Con todo?" Yes, please. On went pineapple and a pinch of cilantro and onion. Underneath went the gray paper and plastic plate.

At the *tlacoyo* stands, women with long gray braids stuffed balls of masa with beans or cheese like an empanada, then pressed it into a oval-shaped patty. The *tlacoyos* cooked on *comales*—a round sheet of metal propped on a square grill—until crisp and freckled on both sides. "Con todo, señorita?" They added diced cactus, onion, cilantro, grated cheese, and a spoonful of salsa.

We moved to Mexico City for my husband's job; I quit my own newspaper job without much of an idea of what I'd do next. We'd both wanted to move to Mexico for years, mostly to improve our Spanish, and I was confident that I'd figure something out—that something turned out to be studying food.

EATING MEXICO FROM BORDER TO BORDER

The neighborhood markets in Mexico City were full of produce I'd never seen before. Huitlacoche, the purplish-gray corn fungus once eaten by the Aztecs, lay in pebbly, damp piles. Fresh cactus paddles sat on mounds of herbs. Clay pots overflowed with cold salads of *nopal* (cactus), *pata* (pig's foot) and *haba* (fava beans). Vendors cried out, "Qué le damos, guerita?" (What can we give you, light-skinned girl?) or "Qué buscaba?" (What are you looking for?) when I walked by. I didn't know whether I was supposed to answer or keep on walking.

In a city that suffered from crippling traffic, crumbling infrastructure, and occasionally fetid air, somehow food was universally adored. Relished, even. *Chilangos*, the local word for people who live in Mexico City, ate on busy avenues and street corners, gulping down tacos, homemade fried potato chips and exhaust. They ate baroque fruit salad sculptures covered in dollops of whipped cream in the markets. They slurped bowls of *barbacoa* consommé on the weekends underneath plastic tarps, and they bought sweet bread from bike-riding vendors.

Residents of Mexico City and the nearby outskirts have created a unique food economy that doesn't exist anywhere else in the country. Immigrants from all over Mexico have flocked to the capital to work, and, depending on the neighborhood and snacks sold, setting up a food business requires relatively little capital. Only in Mexico City can one find food from Puebla, the Yucatán, Oaxaca, Guerrero, Tlaxcala, Baja California and Veracruz, co-existing, side by side. The cuisine of Mexico City historically focused on Central Mexico, but modern Mexico City cuisine boasts a sort of pan-identity, embracing influences and ingredients that extend from Mexico's northern border to Guatemala. It is a chaotic, energizing, and overwhelming place to learn about Mexican food.

Deep down my passion for exploring the tastes of Mexico City was about more than just the food—I was eager to connect with a culture I wanted to know better. My great-grandparents had been born in Sonora, Chihuahua and Guanajuato, but the language and most of the cultural customs hadn't made it to my generation. I had struggled occasionally with my cultural identity in my twenties. Growing close to Mexican food opened up a new door, connecting me to my family and my ancestors in ways I couldn't have predicted.

ABOUT THIS BOOK

This cookbook is an earnest attempt to capture Mexico City's informal food scene, which has continued to fascinate me since those early days in 2009 when I arrived. What this book is *not* is a definitive guide to all of Mexico City's food. There are plenty of well-known local dishes that aren't included here because of time and space constraints. (I'm sorry, *caldo de gallina*.) I'm also hyper-conscious of taking on the herculean task of translating a cuisine that isn't native to me. My sources for the recipes in this book are the same Mexican street, market and *fonda* vendors who've inspired me; collections of popular Mexican recipes (particularly cookbooks by Josefina Velázquez de León); and many other cookbooks and books about Mexican food culture found in Mexico City's lovely Biblioteca de la Gastronomía Mexicana (Library of Mexican Gastronomy) at the Fundación Hérdez in the Centro Histórico.

Many of the recipes in this book require some patience to prepare. There are very few shortcuts in Mexican cooking, which is one of the things I like about it! Early in my time in Mexico City, I took a 14-month cooking course at the Escuela de Gastronomía Mexicana. It was a diploma program solely devoted to Mexican cooking, and during our three- to four-hour weekly cooking and lecture sessions, I tried to suppress the gringa side of me that told me to hurry, hurry, hurry. When preparing Mexican food, it's not about speed or how perfect the plate looks in the end—it's about the steps themselves, and taking pleasure in both the process and the result.

MUST-HAVE MEXICAN INGREDIENTS

Here's a quick guide to the ingredients I use most frequently in this book. You can find these, and many of the other special ingredients used in this book, in Mexican grocery stores or online. Some items may also be found in the Hispanic food aisles of mainstream grocery stores, especially in cities with large Hispanic populations. Throughout the book, I've suggested sources for other hard-to-find ingredients, in some cases Latin, Caribbean, and even Asian markets in the United States.

ANCHO CHILE: A large dried chile with a fruity aroma, the ancho is used most often in moles, adobos and *chiles rellenos*. Sometimes vendors will toss in mulatos with the anchos. To tell them apart, hold an ancho chile up near the light. It should have a reddish tint, possibly near the stem. It also should smell much fruitier than the mulato, which tends to smell more raisiny and prune-like. The ancho is known as a poblano chile when fresh. You can find them in the dried chile section at Mexican grocery stores.

ÁRBOL CHILE (FRESH): A pencil-thin, long green chile, the fresh chile de árbol is consistently hotter than both serranos and jalapeños, which can be forgettable depending on the season and where you buy them. You can find fresh árbols in the produce section at most Mexican grocery stores.

ÁRBOL CHILE (DRIED): Skinny, dried árbol chiles are a deep crimson color and about the same length as the fresh chiles, around 3 to 4 inches long. When purchasing, make sure they have their stems intact. If they don't, they could be chile japonés, which has a different flavor profile. Dried chile de árbol is very hot and best used in table salsas—condiments that sit on the table, for drizzling.

ACHIOTE: Annatto seed in English, *achiote* is sold either ground or in seed form. Ground achiote in Mexico City is most commonly premixed with vinegar and spices and packaged in small rectangular bars. These bars are often used for marinades for *taco al pastor* and *cochinita pibil*. In the United States, you can buy the bars or the whole seeds from online grocers or Mexican grocery stores.

BEANS (DRIED): A staple in the Mexican kitchen. Using the best quality beans you can find matters; old beans may not soften during cooking or can have off flavors. Most of the beans called for in this book are black beans or brown pintos—the latter is my substitute for *bayos*, a creamy brown

Mexican bean that's difficult to source dried in the U.S. For most recipes in this book, really any Mexican bean will do. I'd encourage you to try as many varieties as possible. Rancho Gordo is a great source for Mexican beans online.

MEXICAN BAY LEAF: I call for dried Mexican bay leaves (*litsea glaucescens*) in some of my recipes. The flavor is a bit more subtle than the Mediterranean bay leaf, and the leaf itself is narrower. You can find them in the spice aisle at select Mexican grocery stores.

CILANTRO (FRESH): Fresh cilantro (*coriandrum sativum*) is an essential condiment in Mexican cooking, often mixed with onion and added to tacos, or chopped and added to salsas. It should taste sharp and herbal, with wide, flat leaves that are a bit broader and rounder than flat-leaf parsley. Use both the cilantro leaves and stems for maximum flavor.

CHICKEN BROTH: Mexican chicken broth is not the same as the European variety. It tends to be lighter in taste, generally because it's made with only chicken, onion, garlic and perhaps a bay leaf and salt. If you have time to make your own, it's worth it (see page 98). Be careful when using boxed chicken broths from grocery stores—the flavors may be overly chickeny, and they can ruin a good sauce or mole.

CHIPOTLE CHILES (DRIED): Brown and leathery, dried chipotle chiles (known in Mexico City as "*chipotle meco*") are medium-hot and somewhat smoky and often used in salsas or *mole poblano*. They are jalapeños when fresh. You can find them in the dried chile section at Mexican or Latin grocery stores.

CHIPOTLE CHILES EN ADOBO (CANNED): Canned chipotle chiles are spicier than their dried counterparts, since they are smothered in a sauce that's made from additional chiles (usually anchos). They're a bit fruitier than dried chipotles and freeze very well.

MEXICAN CINNAMON: Also known as true cinnamon, Mexican cinnamon (or *cinnamomum verum*) is much more sharp and flavorful than the cassia usually sold in mainstream U.S. supermarkets. You can find it in the spice aisle at Mexican grocery stores.

CORN HUSKS (DRIED): Dried corn husks are essential in making tamales. In Mexican or Latin grocery stores in the United States, the husks are generally sold in packages of flat, thick, triangular-shaped leaves. I find them difficult to fold and truthfully too manicured for my tastes. I much prefer the stacks of husks sold nestled inside each other in round, rectangular packages—they're often sold at the same Mexican grocery stores that sell the flat variety. These rectangular husks have naturally raised edges and are thinner and more papery, which makes them much easier to fold than the flat ones. If you can't find corn husks and are dead-set on making tamales, you can use parchment paper instead, but the flavor and shape will not be the same.

CREMA: A lightly acidic cream made from cow's milk, Mexican *crema* is usually used to cool off hot or astringent flavors, particularly in enchiladas, *chilaquiles*, tacos, or tostadas. *Crema* is sometimes referred to as "sour cream" at Mexican restaurants in the United States, but that's not exactly accurate. American sour cream is much more sour. You'll find *crema* in the dairy case at Mexican or Latin grocery stores. If you can't find it, you can try making Homemade Crema (page 139) or use sour cream thinned out with a little milk.

EPAZOTE: This pungent herb (*dysphania ambrosioides*) is so abundant in Mexico City, market vendors often give it to me for free. When fresh, it has an intense medicinal flavor. (Bonus: It also has anti-parasitic properties.) While fresh epazote is much preferred over dried, the fresh variety sold in the United States can taste quite mild. If you get a mild batch—so mild you can use it as salad greens—keep adding epazote leaves to the dish until the flavor becomes noticeable. You should only eat the leaves, not the stems. Find epazote at Mexican grocery stores, near the other fresh herbs. Any leftovers can be frozen for future use.

GUAJILLO CHILE (DRIED): A medium-hot chile with a thick, maroon-colored skin, the versatile guajillo is one of my favorite dried chiles. Once hydrated and blended, it paints anything it touches a deep red color, and the flavor is subtle and slightly herbaceous. The guajillo is wonderful in table salsas, adobos, moles, and marinades. Be careful when buying them, though—I've seen some U.S. grocery stores mislabel chile colorados as guajillos. Colorados are sweeter, longer in length, and have a lighter, shinier, more berry-colored skin. A true guajillo will have a rounded tip and thick, dark-red matte skin, and it will taste slightly more acidic and complex.

HABANERO CHILE (FRESH): A small, extremely hot chile, the habanero is perhaps the hottest fresh chile found in Mexico. It's very popular in Yucatecan cooking and in the occasional table salsa in Mexico City. You can find it at most Mexican grocery stores in the United States. A Scotch bonnet pepper is an acceptable substitute, although it won't have the same floral perfume as the habanero.

JALAPEÑO PEPPER: Jalapeños in Mexico City are also known as *cuaresmeños*, although they're called jalapeños in other areas of the country, including Xalapa, Veracruz, where the chile originates. (If you have an opportunity to eat the amazing jalapeños of Xalapa, by all means do it!) Sadly, jalapeños in the U.S. often seem to lack flavor. I'd recommend substituting serranos in cases where you want more heat.

LARD: Mexicans have used lard to fry and *guisar* (stew) for generations, and it's still extremely common. I use it with abandon in this book because it produces the best flavor. The lard I'm referring to is either white or a very light brown in color and freshly rendered, and often sold in plastic quart-size containers at Mexican grocery stores or good butcher shops. Avoid the hard, hydrogenated rectangles of lard sold at supermarkets, which are tasteless.

MASA HARINA: This is my catch-all term for dehydrated, nixtamalized corn flour, meaning the corn has been soaked and cooked in an alkaline solution such as limewater. Fresh masa tastes better every time, but if you can't find it, reconstituting this flour with water will offer an acceptable substitute. This flour is sold under several brand names including Maseca, Minsa and Quaker, and you should be able to find at least one of these at mainstream supermarkets. It's important to note that masa made with dehydrated flour will not be as flexible and soft as true masa. If you're making *tlacoyos* or *huaraches* or any other masa snacks—or tamales—it's worth seeking out real masa made from freshly ground, nixtamalized corn. Cornmeal or regular corn flour should not be substituted.

MORITA CHILE (DRIED): This small, hot, very wrinkled chile has a smoky flavor, with slightly fruity undertones. Moritas have more bite than the regular chipotle meco, so they work wonderfully in table salsas. If they're too brittle to slice open and remove the seeds, try softening them on a *comal* or nonstick skillet first.

MULATO CHILE (DRIED): The mulato—a large, flat, dark-purple dried chile—is used most often in moles or meat sauces. It's medium-hot and smells raisiny and prune-like. You can find mulatos at most Mexican grocery stores in the dried chile aisle, or online.

NOPAL: Nopal refers to the prickly pear cactus paddle, which is sold either with spines or (if you're lucky) already cleaned at Mexican supermarkets. Cactus has a natural slime, but it's reportedly very nutritious. If you hate the slime, dice the cactus and cook on the stovetop until tender, then raise the flame and reduce until the slime has evaporated.

ONION, WHITE: All of my recipes call for white onion, unless explicitly stated. They're sharper tasting than yellow or sweet onions, and they are the traditional aromatic in Mexican cooking.

MEXICAN OREGANO: Used in soups, marinades, *guisados*, and more, Mexican oregano (*lippia berlandieri schauer*) isn't related to the sharper, spicier Italian oregano found at U.S. grocery stores. Several states in Mexico actually have their own varieties of oregano, and several sub-varieties. You can find Mexican oregano online or at Mexican grocers.

PASILLA CHILE (DRIED): This long, skinny dark-chocolate colored chile is medium spicy, with a slightly sweet and faintly tobacco-ish aroma. The pasilla is a chilaca chile when fresh; when dried, it is most often used in moles, adobos, salsas, and soups. You can find it in the produce section at select Mexican grocers.

POBLANO CHILE (FRESH): A large, fresh chile, the dark-green poblano is most often used either stuffed or roasted and cut into strips called *rajas*. The poblanos in Mexico tend to be more flavorful and hotter than those found in the U.S. At their peak in the late summer and early fall months, they're peppery and buttery, and a natural complement to ingredients like cheese and cream. You may see them labeled in some Mexican grocery stores in the United States as "fresh pasilla."

QUESO FRESCO: The words "queso fresco" in my recipes refer to a fresh, white, farmer's-style cheese, lightly salty and creamy, found in the dairy case at any Mexican grocery store. If you live near Latin or South American grocers, don't buy Colombian cheese as a substitute—it's much saltier.

QUESO AÑEJO: A catch-all term for a hard, aged cow's milk cheese, queso añejo is most often crumbled onto tacos, enchiladas and more. Not all Mexican grocery stores in the U.S. carry it, although some sell a salty, slightly aged cheese they call Cotija (which unfortunately I can't recommend, having tasted the real Cotija from Michoacán). Substituting another aged cheese such as ricotta salata or Romano works.

SALT: I use kosher, coarse-ground salt because I prefer the flavor over regular table salt. To substitute table salt, which is saltier, start out with less than what's called for in the recipe.

SERRANO CHILE (FRESH): The dark-green serrano is hotter than a jalapeño, but not as hot as a fresh árbol chile. Its bright, grassy flavor is just about perfect in seafood dishes, stews, sauces and salsas. In the United States, the serranos tend to be larger than they are in Mexico. I much prefer their flavor over the sometimes less-hot jalapeño.

MEXICAN SQUASH: A plump variety of zucchini with mottled, greenish-gray skin (sometimes called "gray zucchini"), Mexican squash can be found at most supermarkets. Regular dark-green zucchini is a fine substitute.

TOMATOES: Tomatoes, both fresh and cooked, are a staple in Mexican cooking. All the tomatoes I use in this book, unless specifically noted, are rectangular plum tomatoes, usually the Roma variety. That said, if the recipe calls for raw tomatoes, it's worth seeking out the best, freshest tomatoes you can find. In some areas of the U.S. locating fresh, ripe tomatoes may not be possible, particularly during the winter. If so, canned or grape tomatoes are an acceptable substitute.

TOMATILLOS: Tomatillos are small, acidic fruits wrapped in a papery husk; they're related to the cape gooseberry. You can find them at Mexican grocers in the produce aisle.

TORTILLAS: I use the standard-size corn tortillas sold at most Mexican grocery stores and bodegas in the U.S., measuring between 5½ and 6 inches in diameter. If using smaller tortillas, adjust your portion sizes accordingly.

ESSENTIAL EQUIPMENT

To make the recipes in this book, you'll need a few items that you may not already own.
All can be found online or at large Mexican grocery stores.

BLENDER: The blender is the workhorse of the Mexican kitchen, used to make table salsas, meat sauces, moles, adobos and more. It replaces the much older-school *molcajete* (lava rock mortar and pestle) and *metate* (sloped lava rock tablet and rolling pin), both of which still produce excellent food, but take much longer to do so. Tip: If you're loading the blender with hot food or sauce, place a kitchen towel over the lid and press down firmly to hold the lid in place. Otherwise the top may pop off and you'll find yourself with sauce all over the ceiling.

COMAL: A round, thin sheet of metal or clay, the *comal* conducts an insane amount of heat, which means it's perfect for lightly charring tomatoes for salsas, toasting garlic, or warming several tortillas at a time. A nonstick skillet is a more or less acceptable substitute, but if you think you may be cooking Mexican recipes more than once, a *comal* is worth the modest investment.

LARGE POTS: Many of the recipes in this book call for boiling several pounds of meat at a time, and some call for cooking large cuts of meat slowly in lard. It's helpful to have at least one large, heavy-bottomed (at least 12-quart) pot to be able to cook the dishes such as Carnitas (page 38), Turkey Tortas (page 48), Pozole (page 65), and Mole (page 124). Particularly with mole, a heavier pot is essential, otherwise the mole will stick and burn.

SPICE GRINDER: An electric spice grinder, or a coffee grinder, comes in very handy when making mole, or other sauces or marinades that call for grinding a large number of spices and nuts. For smaller quantities, or times when your sauce may not need to be so velvety smooth, a mortar and pestle work just fine.

STRAINER: A fine-mesh strainer—preferably a large, deep one—is essential for straining the pesky seeds and skin out of tomato sauces; making moles and adobos velvety smooth; straining coffee grains out of Café de Olla (page 61); or even straining out big pineapple chunks from your Tepache (page 63).

TORTILLA PRESS: Unless you're already skilled at patting out tortillas by hand, it's necessary to have a tortilla press on hand to flatten your tortillas to an acceptable thinness. Your other option would be two sheets of grocery-bag plastic and a rolling pin, although tortillas made this way may not come out perfectly circular.

CHAPTER 1

ON THE STREETS

My love for the street food of Mexico City bloomed out of necessity. It was 2009, my second week in town, and as I made my way along the sidewalks, I found myself growing progressively weak, my growling stomach about to chomp through my intestines. My health-conscious American gringa side—the same side that had enrolled in fitness bootcamps for two years—told me to buy a granola bar at a convenience store. But I didn't want a granola bar. Not when I had fried meat smells coming at me from all directions. I found a taco stand, bought something with meat, drizzled it with salsa and scarfed it down, ignoring the inner voice that warned I'd regret it.

Now, I still eat on the street at least once a week when I'm in Mexico. I love the sense of community and ritual involved, and the feeling of comfort amid the chaos of the streets. Upon arrival, customers always say "Buenos días" or "Buenas tardes." Folks who are about to leave tell the others to enjoy their meal—*provecho*—while the remaining eaters chorus back "Gracias!" (I have several times choked down bites of taco just to say "Gracias!") Most street stands offer small comforts: plastic overturned buckets or stools to sit on—old ladies always get first dibs—and if not napkins, squares of gray paper to wipe your hands.

Street food breaches many of Mexico City's socio-economic boundaries, but there's a general conception that it's not fit for the wealthy class. Foreigners aren't prone to wandering the city's blue-collar neighborhoods, so it may seem a little strange to *chilangos* that my favorite place to walk and observe is Calle López, a dirty, pothole-ridden street about a block west of Eje Central. The area is technically considered the Centro Histórico, but it is not the Centro Histórico frequented by tourists. Crumbling Art Deco apartment buildings share the landscape with dozens of raw chicken vendors and small kitchens selling cheap home-style cuisine. There is an egg shop, a *tortillería*, a handful of taco stands, a market and some kitchen stores.

The upscale Mercado San Juan, where Mexico City's top chefs buy their groceries, lies just down the street.

Calle López doesn't really wake up until ten a.m., when the *fondas* begin emitting cooking smells, and pots of chicken stock and deep-red sauces bubble on stoves. Women from far-flung pueblos in the State of Mexico arrive and lay down their edible merchandise on the sidewalk, squeezing into an uneven space next to a row of parked cars. During lunch hour, it's nearly impossible to walk freely. Across from the San Juan Arcos de Belén Market, petite sidewalk delis offer tortillas, cooked vegetable *guisados,* and produce trucked in from local farms. A woman with gray braids tied with a black ribbon hand-pats tortillas and *tlacoyos* and lays them gently on the *comal,* while another woman further down the block stands in front of a clay cauldron of rust-red chorizo, spooning it into corn tortillas.

The largest street food stands in the neighborhood lie at the head of Calle López and a narrower street named Aranda. By two p.m., this area—essentially a large patch of concrete, shaded by plastic tarps—blares full blast. Horns shriek and tubas thump from an unseen radio. A man's loudspeaker voice declares that one herbal supplement will solve all your health woes. A breeze lifts the air from the sewers, mixes in odors of grease and cilantro, and tosses the cocktail up your nose.

Many of the sidewalk stands on Calle López are staffed by women. I have tried to get to know them, but many are suspicious of people asking too many questions. Then one afternoon, Maria Luisa Gonzalez, a stout, middle-aged woman with a thick black braid and the standard female street vendor's checkered smock opened up to me. She's staffed her sidewalk stand for six years; someone from her town has held the location for more than fifty.

Gonzalez sells homemade foods prepared by her sister, arranging bowls of cactus and fava bean salads, stewed greens, platters of *chiles rellenos*, cauliflower fritters, and homemade blue and white corn tortillas. Like other vendors in this area, she does not live in the neighborhood; she lives in San Francisco Xochicuautla, located about halfway between Mexico City and Toluca. She wakes up at four a.m. every day to make it to the stand by nine thirty.

Mexico City officials have tried to clean up parts of the Centro, sweeping away the street vendors near the Zócalo, or public square, and even bringing in police with plastic riot shields to prevent any sellers from coming back. But the Calle López vendors remain, mostly undisturbed.

One vegetable stand near the corner of López and Delicias looks like it hasn't changed in fifty years. A table barely larger than a TV tray displays items of food as if they were jewels. Twenty-carat-sized habaneros sit next to a bundle of six serrano peppers, a pyramid of three thin-skinned criollo avocados, and one lonely bunch of herbs. The woman who operates the stand never greets me when I walk by and stare. She knows my favorite thing to do is look.

TORTILLAS DE MAÍZ
HOMEMADE CORN TORTILLAS

In one of my first cooking classes in Mexico City, we students crowded around a *comal*, watching our baby tortillas puff up into starchy yellow bubbles.

Someone said, "Mira, se infló! Ya te puedes casar." (Look it inflated! Now you can get married.)

It was a joke, an old wives' tale, but the implication stuck with me: tortillas were an important part of the Mexican diet, but how you make them, your skill, mattered too.

As a gringa learning how to make Mexican food in Mexico, I could not ignore the tortilla, even if I was happily married. I studied the history of corn and spent two and a half hours in class grinding my own masa on the *metate*, an ancient lava-rock tablet and rolling pin. I took extra tortilla-making classes, and befriended a lovely woman who ran a *tortillería* in the Centro Histórico. She didn't mind when I peppered her with questions about where the corn and the masa came from, and how the tortilla machine worked.

In urban Mexico City, the tradition of making corn tortillas has not changed much in at least a few hundred years. The dough is ground by volcanic stone in corn mills now, not by women hunched over a *metate*, but it is still ground fresh daily. (Although fluctuating corn prices mean that many *tortillerías* now used dried nixtamalized corn flour instead of fresh corn.) Every day around one or two p.m., people queue up to buy their portion, clutching dish towels to wrap their tortillas and take them home.

Since corn and masa are so integral to the Mexican diet—they've been eaten for millennia—it's worth it to make your own fresh masa at least once in your life, just to witness the journey from kernel to dough. You can find dried corn for making tortillas online (don't use popcorn!), or you can buy some in Mexico and bring it back in your suitcase.

To grind the corn at home, I like a tabletop electric mill such as the Nixtamatic, which is designed specifically for nixtamal. Unfortunately, it's currently only sold in Mexico. Some *tortillerías* in the United States may also grind your nixtamal for a fee—if you live in a city with a large Mexican population, it's a question worth exploring. A third option would be using a hand-cranked mill designed specifically for wet-grinding corn, such as a Corona or Victoria model (both sold online). You may need to pass the masa through a few times to reach the desired smooth texture.

As someone who's made dozens of sticky, too-thick, too-thin, burnt, raw, dry, and gummy tortillas, I can definitively say that there is no magical set of instructions that will get you perfect tortillas every time. A steady, hot heat is important, as is well-kneaded, hydrated masa. But I still stand over the *comal* with a furrowed brow, willing the tortillas to puff up. Sometimes they don't and that's okay. This is a lifelong journey—for Mexicans and anyone seeking to truly understand their cuisine.

HACIENDO TORTILLAS
MAKING TORTILLAS

1½ cups masa harina or 1 pound tortilla masa, ground
    from fresh nixtamal (page 25)
1 cup plus 2 tablespoons warm water

1 If using masa harina, place in a large, deep bowl and slowly add the water. Knead into a moist, cohesive dough that cleanly pulls away from the bowl and no longer feels sticky or thin, about 3 minutes. To test whether the masa is adequately hydrated, grab a piece, roll it into a ball, and flatten it. If the sides crack, the masa needs more water. The final texture should be slightly damp, like cold clay. Once the masa is ready, cover it with a damp dishcloth and let rest 15 minutes, which will result in a softer, more pliable dough.

2 If using fresh tortilla masa, sprinkle a little water, a tablespoon at a time, onto the masa and knead firmly until soft and pliable. You should need ¼ cup water at the most, depending on how dry and crumbly the masa is.

3 Heat a *comal* or nonstick skillet to medium-low heat.

4 Break off a knob of masa and roll it into a smooth ball, about the size of a golf ball. Cover the rest of the dough with a damp dishcloth.

5 Flatten the dough ball between your palms, so it's about ½ inch thick. Place on one side of a tortilla press lined with square sheets of plastic (these can be cut from plain grocery bags but avoid those with lettering or illustration as the coloring could leach onto the tortillas). Make sure the dough circle sits smoothly between the plastic sheets, then close the press. Push down the lever. (See photos on page 24.)

6 Open the press and rotate the tortilla a quarter-turn, keeping the sheets intact. Close and push down on the lever again. Continue to rotate the tortilla until it's evenly pressed into a round about ⅛-inch thick. (If you have a heavy press that will make a thin, even tortilla every time, you can skip the rotating routine.)

7 Open the tortilla press and peel back the top plastic sheet. Place the tortilla face down in your open palm, so about half of it sits in the center of your hand, the other half hanging off.

Gently peel back the remaining plastic sheet. The dough should not stick to the plastic or your hands. If it does, you've added too much water and need to start over. (See "Troubleshooting Homemade Corn Tortillas" on page 24.)

8 Thicker tortillas will be easy to place on the *comal*. Tortillas made with fresh masa, however, take some practice. With half the tortilla resting in your open palm, and the other half hanging off the side, stand over the *comal* and slowly move your hand in a horizontal fashion, spreading the tortilla so the underside hits the *comal* first.

9 Flip—with a heatproof spatula or your callused fingers— as soon as the outer edges of the tortilla start to darken and look less moist, about 45 seconds. The tortilla should have some dark-brown freckles at this point. If it doesn't, raise the heat. Alternately, if it's blackened, lower the heat.

10 Flip the tortilla again as soon as small air bubbles start to appear on the freckled surface, about 35 seconds. At this point, after the second flip, the tortilla might inflate. Cook the tortilla for another 25 seconds, and then push it to the side of the *comal*, away from hot direct heat, and cook 25 seconds more. Flip once more and cook for another 45 seconds, for a total of roughly 3 minutes per tortilla, depending on how hot your stove is. Place the tortilla in a dishcloth or covered basket to keep warm.

11 Repeat steps 4 through 10. Serve the tortillas warm and store any leftovers in an airtight container in the refrigerator for up to a week, or alternately, freeze for longer storage. To reheat, place thawed tortillas on a *comal*, or reheat individually on a gas burner.

COOKING TIP: Cal, *the Spanish word for calcium oxide, is an alkaline solution needed for nixtamalizing corn. In Mexico you can occasionally find it in rock form, but in the U.S. it's generally white and powdery, and available in small packets at Mexican grocers.*

TROUBLESHOOTING HOMEMADE CORN TORTILLAS

Be aware that masa made from masa harina, and masa made from fresh nixtamal do not feel the same. Masa composed from dehydrated flour is stiffer and denser; because of that, it is more difficult to press a thin tortilla with masa harina. Just be patient and persistent, and do the best you can.

If you're using masa harina and the resulting dough is too sticky, sprinkle a little more masa harina on top and knead until smooth and moist. Try to make another tortilla and see if it sticks to your hands or the plastic; if it does, you need a bit more.

If you're making your own nixtamal, the kneading may take much longer, 15 to 20 minutes, to reach the desired soft texture. Grinding your own nixtamal also requires more water, around 1 cup for 3 pounds of freshly ground dough.

If you buy fresh tortilla masa from a tortillería, the dough must be kneaded before shaping it into tortillas. Add a few drops of water, kneading until you have a soft, airy, dough. For tlacoyos or huaraches, add more water as they take longer to cook and they'll dry out if not sufficiently hydrated.

The water temperature does matter. When making tortillas with masa harina, warm water results in a more malleable, pliable dough. Cold or room temperature water is fine for fresh masa.

It's impossible to overknead tortilla dough. So go ahead. Get your aggressions out as you knead, or peacefully stare into the middle distance.

Dividing the masa into individual balls first may dry it out, even if it's sitting under a damp dish towel. Instead I like to knead the masa with damp hands, and pull off portions as needed, as they do on the streets.

Most tortillerías in Mexico City do not add salt to their masa, so I don't salt mine either. I don't miss it, particularly since I often add salsa to whatever I'm eating with the tortillas anyway.

The printed instructions on bags of masa harina are not always correct. Using visual and tactile cues is much more reliable.

FRESH NIXTAMAL

This makes quite a bit of masa—around 3 pounds—but if making fresh nixtamal is new for you, you'll want to have some leftover dough for use later. I prefer to freeze extra dough in 1-pound balls, in sealed plastic bags, or, if I have a friend on hand to help, we'll make tortillas or tlacoyos and freeze those. Masa or frozen tortillas should last at least a few months in the freezer, tightly sealed.

1 Pick over the corn carefully, removing any stones or bits of matter.

2 Pour the water into a large pot. Add the calcium oxide and stir until dissolved. Bring this mixture to a vigorous boil.

3 Stir in the corn, making sure it does not stick to the bottom. Lower the flame to medium, and simmer until the outer skin of the corn barely scrapes off with your fingernail, 7 to 10 minutes. The corn will still be hard at this point. Do not overcook it or else your masa will be too gummy.

4 Remove the pot from the heat and cover. Let sit at least 6 hours or overnight.

5 The next day, drain the corn. Wash the kernels well, rubbing them between your hands to loosen and discard any errant skins. This may take 5 to 10 minutes, depending on how many of the skins came loose in the pot.

6 At this point the corn is ready to be ground, either by hand or at a local mill. (The kernels must be cool or room temperature in order to do so.) Once the corn has been ground into tortilla masa, it must be sufficiently hydrated and kneaded (see "Troubleshooting Homemade Corn Tortillas" opposite for detailed instructions). Then the masa is ready to be shaped into tortillas.

2 pounds dried corn for making tortillas/masa

3 quarts cold water

1 tablespoon plus 1 teaspoon powdered calcium oxide, also known as *cal*

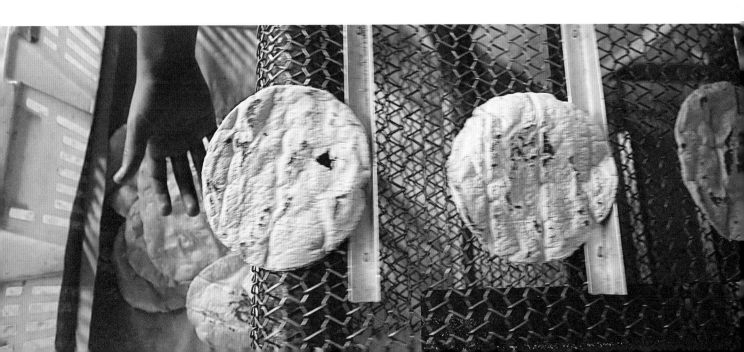

SALSA VERDE CRUDA
RAW TOMATILLO SALSA

Green salsas run the gamut on Mexico City streets. They can be boiled, pea green and soupy; they can be charred and thick and flecked with blackened bits of tomatillo. They can also be astonishingly hot, which is why it's always good to ask the street vendor, "Cuál salsa pica más?" (Which salsa is hotter?) This is my favorite version of all: a raw, acidic, chunky purée that slices through anything fatty; I like to serve it with Slow-cooked Pork (page 38), Crispy Carrot Tacos (page 115), Tlacoyos (page 42), Mexican-style Eggs (page 86), and almost anything else.

9 fresh árbol chiles, or
    4 to 5 serrano chiles
1 large garlic clove, peeled
10 ounces tomatillos, husked and
    rinsed (see below)
2 tablespoons cold water
¼ cup plus 2 tablespoons diced
    onion
1 tablespoon chopped cilantro,
    or more to taste
juice of ½ large lime, optional
½ teaspoon salt, or more to taste
½ medium Hass avocado, diced,
    optional

1   Chop the chiles and garlic roughly, and place in a blender jar. Blitz until mostly chopped.

2   Cut the tomatillos in half and add to the blender jar with the water. Liquefy until the salsa transforms into a thick, chunky sauce.

3   Pour into a bowl and stir in the onion and cilantro. Taste and see if you like it as is, or if you'd prefer more acidity or salt. If so, add the lime juice and taste again. Then stir in the salt and taste one more time, adding more salt, if necessary. Top with the avocado, if using, just before serving.

4   Salsa (minus the avocado) keeps for about a week in a sealed container in the fridge.

VARIATION: *To make another version of green salsa that's typical of street stands, blend the avocado with the onion and cilantro. Then taste for lime juice and salt, and blend again.*

COOKING TIP: *As with every salsa in Mexico, it's really the cook's touch that gives it personality. Feel free to add more water if you want it thinner, and—even though some Mexicans probably wouldn't agree—you can even omit the salt, which creates a brighter, sweeter salsa that's almost like a relish. If you own a powerful blender, no need to chop anything first. Just toss it in the blender jar whole.*

HOW TO BUY AND PREPARE TOMATILLOS

Small tomatillos, occasionally labeled miltomates in Latino grocery stores, tend to be more flavorful than the larger ones. In Mexico City cooks generally use the larger tomatillos, known as tomate verde, in sauces and smaller tomatillos in table salsas.

Choose tomatillos that are firm and not loose in their husks. While bright yellow and hunter-green criollo varieties are available in Mexico, elsewhere around the world the tomatillos should be a light lime-green color, or perhaps lime green splotched with purple. Avoid tomatillos that look wrinkly or pale and colorless. It's best to buy a bit more than you think you'll need, as you may discard a few later.

To clean, remove the husk and rinse in water to scrub off any dirt. Some cooks in Central Mexico reserve the husks and boil them in water with tequesquite, a type of salt that grows on the highland lakes that is also traditionally used as a leavening agent for tamales instead of baking powder.

SALSA ROJA TAQUERA
RED TACO-STAND STYLE SALSA

The best red salsas I've had on the street are a deep, rusty brick color, and they taste definitively of dried chiles, acid and salt. Most people use a combination of dried árbol chiles—the hottest dried chile in the markets—and guajillo or cascabel, which paint the salsa a gorgeous deep-red color. In this simple version, I keep the tomatoes to a minimum and omit onion, so the chiles can shine brighter. It's tongue-swellingly hot, which makes it perfect on just about anything. I've called for eight dried árbol chiles, but you can bump it up to ten for even more fire.

1   Snip off the stems of the chiles and shake out their seeds as best you can. If the chiles are too dry and brittle, warm them slightly on a gently heated *comal*, and then remove the seeds. Alternately, keep the seeds in to make a very hot salsa.

2   Heat the *comal* on low to medium-low and place the unpeeled garlic cloves near the edge of the pan, away from direct heat. Turn occasionally until soft and blackened in spots, 5 to 7 minutes. Peel the garlic cloves once cool enough to handle and set aside in a blender jar.

3   To toast the chiles, work with one at a time so they don't burn. Place each chile near the edge of the *comal*—again, away from the hottest part of the pan—and turn constantly for 5 to 10 seconds, pressing any wrinkled or folded spots lightly so all parts of the chile skin come into contact with the pan. They are done when the color lightens up in spots and they emit a spicy aroma. (This is a very quick process!) Remove all toasted chiles to a separate bowl and cover with water. Let sit 15 minutes or until the skins are soft. Reserve the soaking water.

4   While the chiles sit, heat the *comal* to medium or medium-high. Cook the whole tomatoes, turning often with tongs, until soft and blackened in spots. Transfer to a bowl and set aside.

5   Add the hydrated chiles to the blender jar (with the garlic), with 2 tablespoons of the reserved chile water and a generous ¼ cup water. Blend until smooth. Add the tomatoes and 2 tablespoons more water, plus ¾ teaspoon salt. Blend again, adding more water and salt if desired. (Note that the saltiness will mute when the still-warm salsa cools.) Serve at room temperature.

8 to 10 dried árbol chiles
2 guajillo chiles
3 medium cloves garlic, unpeeled
2 ripe plum tomatoes
salt

COOKING TIP: *Just make sure you choose real guajillos and not, as can occasionally happen in the United States, colorados mislabeled as guajillos. The thinner-skinned colorados will make the salsa taste too sweet, and the color won't be as deep red; see page 12 in the Ingredients section.*

Whether you use a blender or a molcajete *(a lava-rock mortar and pestle)*, it's easy to start creating your own homemade salsas. Salsas are generally comprised of four things:

- Dried or fresh chiles
- Aromatics, such as garlic or onion
- Acids, such as tomatoes, tomatillos, or lime juice
- Salt

All of these items, save for the salt of course, can be prepared in the following ways: roasted on a comal or nonstick skillet, boiled, or used raw. At that point they can be chopped, mashed in a molcajete or blended. The combinations are endless, particularly when you start adding in things like fresh herbs, peanuts, or other native Mexican ingredients like xoconostles or guaje seeds.

Here are some more guidelines to follow:

- Taste as you go, so you can see how the flavors stack up along the way.

- Good salsa needs salt. If your batch of salsa lacks oomph, add a hefty pinch of salt and taste again.

- Warm ingredients amplify the saltiness. You have to wait until a salsa reaches room temperature to truly know what it tastes like.

- Good salsa needs acid. So you've salted it, but it's still flat and boring. Does it need lime juice? Maybe a spurt of vinegar?

- If you lack a high-powered blender, blend garlic or onion and chiles first. This helps you control the texture later on, particularly if you're creating a salsa with chunky bits of tomatoes or tomatillos, which break down quickly in a blender. Likewise, if you're working in a molcajete, mash the aromatics first—they'll break down the easiest, and they'll impart a flavorful coating for the later ingredients.

SALSA DE CHILE DE ÁRBOL CON CACAHUATE
ÁRBOL CHILE AND PEANUT SALSA

Peanut salsas aren't exactly common on the street, but you can find them at the more creative stalls and taquerías. With so much competition, a taco stand truly is only as good as its salsas. The fried peanuts in this salsa lend a silky texture, backed up by a killer combo of fried garlic and vinegar. It's great on any taco, roasted vegetables, eggs, potatoes, or dipped with homemade tortilla chips. This salsa is hottest when eaten within a few days. After that, the flavor mellows considerably.

1 In a medium skillet, heat the oil over medium-low heat. Fry the árbol chiles first, turning often with tongs until they soften, toast, and start to release a spicy aroma, 1 to 3 minutes, trying not to burn them so they'd don't impart a bitter flavor. Remove to a bowl and then fry the guajillos, cooking until the skin puffs up, shines and brightens in color. Transfer to the same bowl.

2 Fry the peanuts in the same pan, stirring constantly, until they toast to an even golden brown on all sides, 3 to 4 minutes. (If you notice them start to burn or blacken in spots, lower the flame.) Transfer to the same bowl as the chiles.

3 Raise the heat to medium. Fry the garlic cloves in the same skillet until blistered and dark golden on all sides. Transfer to the bowl.

4 Cut the chiles into smaller pieces. Put the chile mixture in a blender jar, discarding any leftover oil. Add the water, salt and vinegar. Blend on high until very smooth and silky, at least 2 or 3 minutes. Serve at room temperature. Refrigerate any leftovers in an airtight container.

1 tablespoon canola oil

10 dried árbol chiles, stemmed and seeded

7 guajillo chiles, stemmed and seeded

2 tablespoons raw unsalted peanuts

2 medium cloves garlic, peeled

1¼ cups plus 2 tablespoons water

2½ teaspoons salt

3 to 4 teaspoons apple cider vinegar, or more to taste

CEBOLLAS ENCURTIDAS
PICKLED ONIONS AND HABANERO

Pickled onions are a must-have condiment on any street taco, although they're probably best known at the tacos de canasta stands and Yucatecan-style fondas that serve cochinita pibil (page 121). The power duo of habaneros and vinegar marries perfectly with anything greasy, while the raw onion adds crunch. Another bonus: they don't take long to make. This tastes best if left in the refrigerator overnight before eating. You can store these for at least a week.

1 Slice the onion into slivers, place in a medium bowl and cover with boiling water. Let sit for 10 minutes, then drain.

2 Return the onions to same bowl and add the remaining ingredients. Cover with an airtight lid and let sit at least 2 hours, or even better, overnight, before serving.

COOKING TIPS: *Feel free to add more habaneros if you want more heat, or substitute the larger Scotch bonnet pepper if you can't find them. Just don't touch your eyes, nose, or mouth after handling.*

1 medium onion

½ cup white vinegar

2 large habanero chiles, stemmed, seeded, and sliced into slivers

½ teaspoon dried thyme

¼ teaspoon dried Mexican oregano

1 teaspoon salt

⅛ teaspoon ground black pepper

QUESADILLAS DE HONGOS
MUSHROOM QUESADILLAS

Mushrooms stewed in garlic, chile, and epazote are a fixture at the tlacoyo *and quesadilla stands that set up along city sidewalks. The vendors, most often women, make their stews—also known as* guisados—*the day before at their homes, and then bring them to work in plastic containers. The food sells out most often around four p.m. The epazote in this recipe is key. The bitter herb, which grows like a weed in Mexico City (you sometimes actually see it sprouting from sidewalks), has a distinct flavor that for me encapsulates Central Mexican cooking. Serve these with a salsa of your choice.*

1 pound crimini mushrooms
2 medium cloves garlic, minced
1 serrano chile, minced with
    seeds
2 tablespoons olive oil
¼ large onion, chopped
¼ teaspoon salt
¼ cup chopped fresh epazote
    leaves
4 to 8 ounces Monterey Jack or
    other mild, meltable cheese,
    grated
8 to 12 corn tortillas

COOKING TIPS: *The epazote I've bought in New York tends to be less pungent than the Mexican variety, so I've added quite a bit here. I've also browned the mushrooms, something the vendors don't normally do, as they make their fillings the night before.*

1   Rub any dirt from the mushrooms with a damp paper towel. Do not discard the stems. Slice mushrooms into ⅛-inch pieces.

2   In a small bowl, mix together the garlic and chile and set aside.

3   Pour 1 tablespoon oil into a large, deep skillet and heat to medium-high. Add half of the onion and cook until translucent, about 3 minutes. Add half of the garlic and chile mixture and cook, stirring constantly, until aromatic and slightly soft, about 1 minute.

4   Stir in half of the mushrooms, tossing in the oil to coat. Lower the heat slightly so the garlic doesn't burn, and cook undisturbed for at least 2 minutes until the mushrooms begin to release their juices. Raise the heat to high and cook until the mushrooms turn a darker golden brown on one side, 4 to 5 minutes. Carefully stir and cook until both sides are evenly browned and most of the moisture has evaporated.

5   Stir in half the salt and epazote, then transfer the mixture to a bowl while you cook the second batch.

6   Create a workspace near the stove with the mushrooms, cheese and tortillas at the ready. Warm a large (10- to 11-inch) *comal* or nonstick skillet over medium heat. Line with three tortillas. Heat the tortillas, flipping perhaps three or four times, until soft and pliable. Transfer to your workspace.

7   Place 3 to 4 tablespoons cheese on one side of the tortilla, plus about 2 heaping tablespoons of mushrooms. Fold over into a half-moon shape and return each quesadilla to the *comal*, with the cheese side closest to the heat. Press down on each with a heatproof spatula for about 10 seconds, so they stay closed.

8   Flip the quesadillas once the underside has turned slightly crispy and freckled in parts, after 2 to 3 minutes. (If they burn, turn the heat down slightly; conversely, if they are still limp after 3 to 4 minutes, turn the heat up.) Cook until crisp and melty, about 4 minutes total. Tip: If the *comal* is very hot, move the quesadillas after the initial few flips to the outer edges of the pan, away from direct heat.

9   Serve immediately, or transfer to the oven, warmed at the lowest setting, until all the quesadillas have been cooked.

HUITLACOCHE QUESADILLAS
CORN SMUT QUESADILLAS

Huitlacoche (wheat-lah-COE-chay) is the Nahuatl-derived word for the puffy, purplish-blue fungus that grows on top of corn. It's widely eaten in Mexico City and the surrounding states, where it's most often spooned into quesadillas or crepes. Huitlacoche is at its peak during the rainy season (June to September), when suddenly buckets of it pop up in local markets. The best kind is light in color and free of any black mold. The flavor mixes the earthiness of mushrooms with the slight sweetness of corn. Serve these with a salsa of your choice. The cheese is up to you as well—in Mexico I use Chihuahua, which is mild and melty, but in the U.S. good-quality Chihuahua cheese is hard to find. Monterey Jack makes a good substitute.

1   Heat the oil in a medium skillet over medium-high heat. Add the onion and cook until translucent, about 3 minutes. Add the garlic and chile, and cook until the garlic starts to release its aromas, about 1 minute.

2   Stir in the corn, huitlacoche, ½ cup water and salt to taste. Lower the heat slightly, cover, and cook, stirring occasionally, until the corn and huitlacoche are both tender, about 10 minutes. If the corn is not tender and all the liquid has evaporated, add more water and keep cooking. (Alternatively, if the corn is tender and the mixture appears soupy, raise the heat to high and reduce the liquid.) Add more salt to taste and remove from the heat.

3   Heat a large, heavy skillet or *comal* over medium heat. Place a plate and the cheese nearby. Warm a few tortillas at a time, depending on the size of your pan, until soft and pliable. Remove to the plate and place about ¼ cup shredded cheese on one side of each tortilla, and add 2 heaping tablespoons of filling to each. Fold over into a half-moon shape and return to the hot *comal*. Press down for perhaps 20 seconds with the underside of a spatula (or your hand) until each quesadilla keeps its shape. Cook, flipping 3 or 4 times, until both sides are lightly crisp—I actually like mine very crisp—and the cheese is oozy and melty, 4 to 5 minutes. If the *comal* is very hot, move the quesadillas after the initial few flips to the outer edges of the pan, away from direct heat.

4   Repeat with the remaining tortillas, cheese and filling.

5   Serve right away, or transfer to the oven, warmed at the lowest setting, until all the quesadillas have been cooked.

3 teaspoons canola oil
½ heaping cup chopped onion
1 large garlic clove, minced
½ to 1 serrano chile, minced with seeds
1 cup fresh corn kernels
1 pound fresh huitlacoche (see Tip)
salt
12 corn tortillas
4 to 8 ounces Monterey Jack or Chihuahua cheese, grated

COOKING TIP: *Fresh huitlacoche may be available in some areas of the U.S., but at this point it's still rare outside Mexico. Musky, gloppy canned huitlacoche tastes nothing like the real thing, so please don't use it as a substitute. Higher-quality huitlacoche in jars is just starting to enter the gourmet food market and is a more flavorful option, if you don't have access to fresh.*

CHICKEN TINGA
CHICKEN IN CHIPOTLE-TOMATO SAUCE

This is another one of those classic guisados, or stewed mixtures, sold at local quesadilla and tlacoyo stands. Shredded chicken is simmered in a light tomato sauce with a touch of smoky chipotle. Usually it's served in a warm, freshly made corn tortilla, with or without cheese. The dish originated in the state of Puebla, but it's become popular in Mexico City and the surrounding states. I've included a tostada version here, which is a bit more fun to eat. Of course, a warm corn tortilla works just as well, too.

1   Remove any excess fat from the chicken breasts, including the skin. Place in a large heavy pot and just cover with cold water. Add the onion, bay leaf and garlic and bring to a boil. Turn the flame to the lowest it will go, cover and simmer for about 25 minutes, or until the chicken is thoroughly cooked. Remove from the pot and let cool. Shred the meat into pieces with your fingers. Strain the broth, reserving 1 cup, and freeze the rest.

2   Make the sauce. If using fresh tomatoes, cut in half and remove the seeds, then coarsely chop. If using canned tomatoes, drain them well, then pulse in a food processor into coarse, chunky pieces. Drain again if they're very juicy.

3   In a large skillet, heat the oil over medium-high heat. When hot, add the onion and cook until soft and translucent, 3 to 5 minutes. Stir in the garlic and cook until aromatic, 30 to 60 seconds. Add the tomatoes, cooking for about 5 minutes if using fresh (you want a thick, chunky paste) or about 3 minutes for canned to let the flavors meld, stirring occasionally.

4   Stir in the shredded chicken, chipotle and adobo sauce, oregano, chicken stock and ½ teaspoon salt. (If using fresh tomatoes, you'll need to add more than ¼ cup stock so the *tinga* doesn't stick to the bottom of the pan as it cooks.

5   The chipotle should be noticeable but not too punchy. Taste and add more if necessary. Bring to a boil, then lower the heat, cover and simmer for about 10 minutes. Uncover and add salt to taste. If the *tinga* still looks soupy, raise the heat and reduce the juices a bit more.

6   To serve as tostadas, slather a thin layer of crema on each tortilla. (For more amped-up chipotle flavor, mix a little of the adobo sauce in the crema.) Add a few spoonfuls of *tinga*, a slice of white onion and two slivers of avocado to each. Top with the crumbled cheese.

VARIATION: *Oyster mushrooms are a great vegetarian substitution here, although mushroom tinga is not necessarily authentic to the streets of Mexico. Prepare the tinga the same way, using 1 pound oyster mushrooms, shredded into strips, and substituting ½ cup vegetable broth or water. Leave the lid off while cooking and turn the heat up after about 5 minutes to reduce some of the juices.*

2 pounds bone-in chicken breasts
¼ small onion
1 dried Mexican bay leaf
1 medium garlic clove, unpeeled

For the *tinga* sauce:

6 ripe plum tomatoes, or 1 (32-ounce) can whole, peeled tomatoes
1 tablespoon canola oil
1¼ cups chopped onion
1 medium garlic clove, minced
2 chipotles en adobo from a can, minced, with seeds, plus 2 teaspoons adobo sauce, or more as needed
½ teaspoon Mexican oregano
¼ cup Basic Homemade Chicken Stock (page 98), plus more if needed
salt
2 cups Homemade Crema (page 139)
12 tostadas or tortillas
1 onion, sliced
1 avocado, peeled, pitted, and sliced
queso añejo or another aged, crumbly cheese

BASIC SAVORY COARSE-GROUND MASA FOR TAMALES

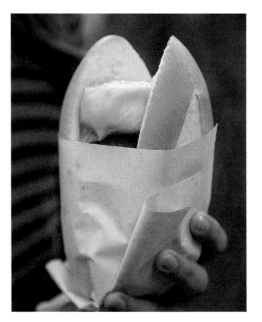

Tamales in Mexico City are notoriously dense with masa, the idea being that such a substantive meal will stave off hunger for hours. Tricycle-riding vendors sell them just as most commuters are making their way to work, from six to ten a.m. The vendors come back out when the sun sets.

Not all street tamales have the same texture. The city's banana-leaf tamales, an influence from the Gulf Coast and Oaxaca, tend to be smoother and firmer and are made with tortilla masa. Steamed corn-husk tamales are made from tamal masa, a coarse-ground masa that's grainier than the tortilla.

For many Mexico City cooks, coarse-ground masa often starts with dried, nixtamalized corn flour, sold by the kilo in neighborhood markets. Select mills in the city—fewer and fewer, but they still exist—also sell freshly ground nixtamalized corn flour, which feels damp and moist like soil. The latter produces the lightest, fluffiest tamales I've tasted.

Both flours are always hydrated with fat (almost always lard) and broth, which adds flavor and makes them puff up like steamed puddings.

For home cooks inexperienced with masa, making a good batch can rely on several factors: the type of fat you use, whether you whip the lard or simply stir it a few times, whether you're using fresh nixtamalized masa or masa harina, and how much broth you use for both; and even, some Mexican cooks say, whether you're angry when you're making them, which could lead to half-cooked tamales. (In cooking school, we peeled off strips of corn husk and tied bows on the steamer pot handles, so the pot would be happy and our tamales would turn out nicely.)

All of that said, tamales can also be forgiving, in the sense that they'll nuzzle and steam whatever you place inside them. And as a cooking instructor once told me, "They should be eaten out of the husk, or else you don't know how to eat tamales."

This recipe, for a coarse-ground tamal dough, can be used for almost anything you like. Just make sure you incorporate air into the masa. Aerate the lard by whipping it thoroughly first, then incorporate more air as you add the moistened masa bit by bit, which will result in a lighter, fluffier tamal. The tamales will be very soft when you remove them from the steamer. Give them about 15 minutes to firm up before serving.

HACIENDO TAMALES
MAKING TAMALES

1   If using masa harina, whisk the flour together with the baking powder and salt in a large deep mixing bowl. Working first with a spoon or spatula, and then with your hands, gradually add 3 cups of stock, stirring and then kneading lightly, until all the liquid has been absorbed. Set aside and let sit for 10 minutes to allow the liquid to fully soak into the flour. If using fresh masa, moisten the dough with about ¼ cup stock, and knead well until soft and pliable. Add more liquid only if the masa still seems dry. (You will add the baking powder and salt later.)

2   Meanwhile, in a stand mixer with the paddle attachment, whip the lard on medium speed until it's smooth, glossy, and much more aerated, about 5 minutes.

3   With the standing mixer running on high (or using your hands) integrate small, golf ball–size bits of masa into the lard a little at a time, mixing well after each addition, until a cohesive, very sticky dough forms. It should look similar to a thick muffin batter. Add more liquid if the dough looks too dry.

4   If using fresh masa, sprinkle the baking powder and salt onto the dough. Mix well for several more minutes, and taste to see if the masa needs more salt. If so, add and keep mixing until a cohesive, very sticky dough forms. The dough should feel rather light. If it's very heavy and dense, add a little more liquid and a few tablespoons more fat and keep mixing.

5   Store the dough made with masa harina in the refrigerator, tightly covered, for up to 24 hours. Dough made with fresh masa must be used the very same day or it will turn sour. (Masa harina sucks up liquid quickly, so this dough may need a bit more stock before using it if you've stored it for several hours.)

COOKING TIP: *To test whether the dough is ready to place inside the husk, remove a dime-size bit of masa to a cup of water. If it floats, the masa is ready. If it sinks, you should keep mixing, or perhaps add a bit more fat.*

4 cups masa harina, or 3 pounds
   fresh tamal masa
2 teaspoons baking powder
½ teaspoon salt, or more to taste
¼ to 3 cups room-temperature chicken,
   beef, or vegetable stock, depending
   on the type of masa
1⅓ cups lard, plus 2 tablespoons if using
   fresh masa

TAMALES DE RAJAS
ROASTED POBLANO PEPPER TAMALES

In this popular street tamal, stewed strips of jalapeño lie in a bed of savory corn masa, oozy with cheese and bits of stewed tomato. My version doesn't exactly mimic the street version, which counts on the availability of flavorful tomatoes year round. Instead, I char the tomatoes on the comal, *fry the mixture with a good bit of garlic and onion, and mix that directly into the masa. It's not exactly traditional, but it captures the spirit of a tamal that stands on its own. If you prefer less heat, you can use poblano peppers (charred, skinned, seeded and sliced) instead of jalapeños. (Char the jalapeños the same way as poblanos, over an open gas flame.) Serve in the husk, with plenty of salsa.*

36 dried corn husks, plus more if needed

6 large jalapeños, or 3 poblano chiles

9 plum tomatoes, roasted on a *comal* and set aside to cool, or 1 (28-ounce) can diced tomatoes

1 tablespoon olive oil

heaping ¼ cup chopped onion

2 cloves garlic, minced

2 tablespoons chicken or vegetable stock

½ teaspoon salt

¼ teaspoon ground black pepper

1 batch Savory Coarse-Ground Masa (page 34)

8 ounces Monterey Jack, or another mild, melty cheese, cut into 3 × ½-inch pieces

1   Place the corn husks in an 8- to 12-quart pot of warm water to soak, pulling them apart as they soften.

2   Char, seed and peel the jalapeños (see sidebar opposite.) Cut the chiles into slivers, toss with a few pinches of salt, and set aside.

3   Place the tomatoes in a food processor and pulse until chunky. (If you're using winter tomatoes, you'll want to remove any awful-looking white tomato cores.) Drain through a strainer, tapping the edge to remove excess juice. Save juice for another use, such as a Bloody Mary or Michelada, and place the drained tomatoes in a bowl. Set aside.

4   In a large skillet, heat the oil over medium heat. When shimmering, add the onion and stir quickly, cooking until translucent and soft but not browned, 3 to 4 minutes. Add the garlic and stir until aromatic. Pour in the tomatoes, stock, salt and pepper. Bring to a boil, then lower the heat to medium and cook for 5 to 7 minutes, stirring occasionally, until the flavors meld. Let cool to room temperature, then stir the tomato mixture into the masa. At this point, if you made your masa with masa harina, you can reserve the dough for up to 24 hours. Dough made with fresh masa must be used the same day, or it will turn sour.

5   Lift some of the husks out of the pot and shake off excess water. Arrange a workspace with the *rajas* (charred chiles), cheese, masa and moist husks at the ready.

6   The husks will have two ends: one rounded end that curves upward, almost cup-like, and one thin and pointy. Hold the husk with the rounded end toward you. Add about ¼ cup masa to the moist husk and spread it, using the underside of a spoon, into a longish rectangle. The rectangle should be wide enough to enclose the filling, once you add it. The masa should come to about 1 inch from the bottom of the rounded end. As for the pointy-end side, make sure you leave enough room to fold the husk over. It's best to leave at least an index-finger's length of space on that side.

7   Add two or three pieces of the chiles and some cheese. Clutch both sides of the husk and fold them together, so that the masa covers the filling like a little empanada. Pay attention to the natural way the husk folds in on itself; one side usually feels more natural as the "top" fold. The tamal should fold cleanly and securely, and the filling should not drip out. If it does, you've added too much filling. (You can open the husk and add more masa, if so.)

8 Once closed, fold down the narrower end of the corn husk and press along the fold to seal. Make sure there aren't any holes where masa could seep out during cooking. If there are holes, wrap the *tamal* in another leaf. The finished tamal should look elongated, like a slightly flattened sausage (see page 143 for photos). Set aside on a baking sheet and repeat to make about 24 tamales.

9 When you've stuffed and folded all the tamales, add water to the steamer pot and place a coin in the bottom. The coin will rattle when the water starts to boil.

10 Very carefully, using tongs, place the tamales in a loose vertical position in the steamer pot, with the folded sides touching the pot floor. Don't place them too tightly or they won't have room to expand, and they'll turn out too thick and dense. Cover with more husks, then a layer of plastic wrap, then the steamer pot lid. If the pot has a side opening for the purpose of adding water, cover that as well, with aluminum foil.

11 Steam for 50 to 60 minutes on high heat. (At higher altitudes, this may take longer.) Listen to the pot occasionally to make sure the coin keeps rattling. Add more water if the coin is silent, taking extreme care not to dampen the tamales.

12 To check for doneness, remove one tamal from the pot and open the husk. If it peels back cleanly, without sticking, the tamal is done. Let cool for at least 15 minutes before serving.

COOKING TIP: *If you don't have a 10-quart steamer pot, you can use a stockpot outfitted with a heatproof drinking glass or bowl, with a heatproof plate placed snugly on top. It will be difficult to add more water if you use this method, so fill the lower chamber of the "steamer" with plenty of water.*

HOW TO PROPERLY CHAR POBLANO PEPPERS

In Mexico City, charred poblano peppers—known colloquially as "rajas," for the shape in which they're cut—jazz up just about everything they touch. Their grassy, buttery notes pair especially well with cheese, eggs and cream.

Poblanos are rarely eaten raw. They are roasted on a comal, peeled and seeded, then either stuffed or sliced into strips. The best way to char the peppers is on your stovetop, if you have a gas stove. Here's how to do it:

Place the peppers directly on top of a gas burner, turning with tongs until blackened in spots. Be careful not to overcook them, or the flesh, once you remove the skin, will turn slimy.

Place in a dish towel—I've found that three or four fit well in the average kitchen towel—and wrap into a bundle. This forces the chiles to sweat, which makes the skin easier to remove. (Placing them in a plastic bag or even a covered bowl may cause them to overcook; towels let them breathe.) Leave for 15 to 20 minutes.

Working with one chile at a time, slough off the charred skin with the pads of your fingers. Do not run under water; this removes all the fantastic charred flavor. Use a sharp knife to carefully remove the poblanos' stems and inner seeds. If you are preparing chiles rellenos, cut an incision from tip to end, leaving about an inch of space at each end. If you are making rajas, cut the chiles all the way open, and, using a small spoon or paring knife, remove all seeds as well as any stringy veins.

The flesh should still feel somewhat firm, particularly if you're going to cook them later in a guisado or tamal, and retain a dark-green color. If the flesh is greenish-yellow, the chiles are overcooked.

I don't recommend using an oven to roast poblanos, unless you're roasting dozens at a time. The oven blasts them with too much heat and leaches out the flavor. Likewise for the broiler, unless you place the chiles very close to the heat source.

Charring the chiles in a nonstick skillet or comal is an option if you don't have access to a gas stove.

CARNITAS
SLOW-COOKED PORK

I'd been visiting a carnitas *stand in the Colonia Roma for about three years when I finally worked up the courage to ask the owner, Victor Hugo Quiroz Pérez, if he could show me the process from start to finish. He told me to show up at his shop at six a.m. on a weekday morning. At about six thirty, Quiroz appeared from an apartment building door directly adjacent to the* carnitas *stand: "Buenos días!"*

We walked inside the dark shop. The glass display cases in the front lay empty, to be filled later with glistening pig parts. Quiroz washed his hands in a small sink and then walked over to a huge metal cauldron, already filled with a pool of caramel-colored, melted lard, the same lard used to fry yesterday's carnitas. *Once the lard was warm, he put the* vísceras, *or organ meats, in first; then the shoulder, or* espaldilla.

He took a raw pig's head and carefully sliced the skin off. "Esta es la máscara," he said. (This part is the mask.) Using a small blowtorch, he gently burned off any errant hairs from the thin, limp piece of fat. He whacked the head with a cleaver and pried the two halves apart with his hands. They opened with a loud crack, and he scooped out the soft brains with his fingers, to be used in quesadillas later. (Pig brain quesadillas are a delicacy at carnitas *stands.) Quiroz placed the butterflied head softly into the lard. The skin, or* cuero, *would be added 1 hour later, along with the ribs.*

Quiroz learned the carnitas *trade from his Michoacán-born father, which made sense: most* carnitas *in Mexico City are modeled after those in Michoacán, a state whose capital, Morelia, lies about 4 hours away by bus. Chilango* carnitas *are almost always prepared in the same manner: the pork is slow-cooked for several hours in lard, then chopped and served in a warm corn tortilla. The only accompaniments are lime juice and a bright, hot salsa.*

Unfortunately I didn't have time to stay until the meat finished cooking, but Quiroz insisted that there was no magic to the recipe, beyond adding in a little garlic, orange juice and salt. He was right. When I made the recipe at home, I was astonished by how good it was and how little hands-on work was involved.

7 pounds lard (see Tip)
7 pounds pork shoulder
7 cloves garlic, peeled
¼ cup fresh-squeezed orange
    juice, rind of ½ orange
    reserved
2 teaspoons salt
16 to 20 corn tortillas
lime wedges, for serving
Salsa Verde Cruda (page 26),
    or salsa of choice

1 Melt the lard in a 12-quart pot over medium-low heat.

2 Add the pork, making sure the meat is covered with the hot fat (cut it into 3 pieces if need be). Raise the heat and bring to a high boil.

3 Lower the heat to a simmer—the lard should be a bit foamy—and cook for 1½ hours, uncovered. The lard surface should show consistent, small, gentle bubbles; if it doesn't, raise the heat. Conversely, if it bubbles too roughly and begins to crackle, lower the heat.

4 Meanwhile, mash the garlic in a *molcajete* or mortar with about 1 tablespoon of the orange juice. (Or toss the garlic and ¼ cup orange juice into a food processor.) Scrape into a small bowl and set aside.

5 After the meat has cooked for 90 minutes, add the garlic paste, the juiced orange half (rind and all) and the salt.

6 Continue simmering another 90 minutes, for a total cook time of about 3½ hours, or until the meat is tender and falls apart when pierced with a fork. (Note: this may take less than 3 hours if using meat in pieces, rather than one large shoulder.)

7 Transfer the meat to a wire rack set over a baking sheet to cool. Strain the lard, let cool and store in the refrigerator for future use, such as refrying beans.

8 About 10 minutes before serving, warm the tortillas on a *comal* or nonstick skillet. Wrap in a dishcloth to keep warm.

9 Chop the meat against the grain—don't shred, or else it will become chewy—and serve on a platter, accompanied by the tortillas, lots of lime wedges and the salsa.

COOKING TIP: *You may be tempted to use oil instead of lard, but that would make every* carnitas *vendor in Mexico (and me) weep. If you can't find 7 pounds of pork shoulder, you can use less, as long as you use the equal weight of lard.*

QUESADILLAS DE CAMARÓN
SHRIMP QUESADILLAS WITH AVOCADO

Quesadillas in Mexico City come in several shapes, sizes and preparations. Many don't contain cheese, to which most Americans would respond, "Well, isn't that just a taco?" Without delving too much into what constitutes a taco versus a quesadilla on Mexico City's streets (the biggest cues are the size and shape of the tortilla), the truth is that this snack—a fried, crackly shell of shrimp and creamy avocado—makes you forget cheese and the semantic debate all together.

This particular version is inspired by one of my favorite street stands, which, like others, sells variations on popular Gulf Coast dishes: tostadas with fresh seafood, seafood empanadas and caldo de camarón, a spicy, pungent broth made from dried shrimp (and a hangover cure). The trick here is to keep the oil hot, or else the tortillas won't be crisp enough. Serve with a tart, vinegary salsa such as Valentina sauce, or the Árbol Chile and Peanut Salsa (page 29), to cut some of the fat.

1 Place the bay leaf, garlic clove, onion and 2 pinches of salt in a pot of water. Bring to a boil and add the shrimp. Cook briefly—about 30 seconds—until the shrimp has just turned pink and the flesh firms up. (Don't worry about undercooking because you will fry these later.) Discard the aromatics and drain the broth, reserving for future use if desired. Place the shrimp in a bowl and toss with ¼ teaspoon salt and the white pepper.

2 Place a wire rack on a baking sheet in the oven and heat to 250°F, or the lowest setting on your oven. (For people with crazy-hot ovens, you can preheat the oven to 250°F, and then turn it off.)

3 Pour the oil into a deep pot and heat to between 300°F and 320°F. In a 12-quart pot, the oil will come to about 1 inch high; in a smaller 4-quart pot, perhaps 3 inches. The oil is ready when a dime-size piece of tortilla dropped in the pot sizzles and turns golden brown within 20 to 30 seconds. If the tortilla piece turns dark brown, your oil is too hot.

4 While the oil heats, warm three tortillas on a *comal* until soft and easy to fold. (Don't overcrisp them or else they won't fold at all, and the toothpicks won't insert correctly.) Place two to three pieces of shrimp on one side of each tortilla and fold, securing closed with three toothpicks: one at each corner and one in the center.

5 Once the oil is hot enough, add the quesadillas and fry until slightly golden brown on each side, 2 minutes or less, depending on how hot your oil is. Transfer to the wire rack inside the warmed oven. Repeat with the rest of the tortillas and shrimp, frying 2 to 3 quesadillas at a time, depending on the size of the pot.

6 Once all the quesadillas have been fried, peel and seed the avocado and cut into about ¼-inch slices. Cut the rest of the onion into slivers.

7 Let the quesadillas cool slightly, then carefully—taking care not to break the shell—remove the toothpicks and open each slightly, just wide enough to wedge in 4 to 5 slivers of white onion and 1 slice of avocado. Serve immediately with lime and salsa.

1 dried Mexican bay leaf
1 garlic clove, unpeeled
⅛ small onion, the rest sliced
    for garnish
salt
1 pound raw shrimp, peeled and
    cleaned
⅛ teaspoon white pepper
1 to 1½ quarts vegetable oil
12 corn tortillas, or more if using
    smaller shrimp
1 ripe Haas avocado
 lime wedges, for serving
 Valentina sauce or other tart,
    spicy salsa, for serving

TLACOYOS DE FRIJOL Y REQUESÓN
BEAN AND CHEESE TLACOYOS

Tlacoyos are small, flat patties about the size of your hand, made from corn masa that's been stuffed with mashed beans, requesón (a salty, spreadable cheese similar to ricotta) or fava beans, and cooked crisp on a comal. Once you leave Mexico City, tlacoyos take on other shapes and names. In some areas of Puebla, for instance, they're called tlayoyos.

For a long time, my tlacoyo dream was to find a mayora—an older, respected Mexican cook—who could teach me how to make them. In 2013, I finally was able to learn with Señora Rosa Peña Sotres, who graciously invited me into her home and spent a full Sunday teaching me patiently how to stuff and fold. "Ya aprendió!" (You've learned!), she declared, as I placed a small, misshapen tlacoyito on her charcoal-fired comal.

Patting them out by hand isn't easy if you're a beginner, but you'll get it down with practice. It's fun to gather a group of friends and make them con calma (Spanish for "without hurry"), particularly if someone brings the ready-made masa. Don't skimp on the garnishes. If you can't find cactus, which Latino supermarkets generally stock, try shredded raw cabbage or carrots.

1 teaspoon lard
¼ small onion, the rest chopped
   for garnish
1 medium garlic clove, peeled
16 ounces cooked beans (any
   kind will do), with at least
   ½ cup broth reserved, or 1
   (15.5-ounce) can beans, liquid
   drained and reserved
salt
1 pound fresh tortilla masa,
   or 1½ cups masa harina
1 to 1½ cups warm water
1 cup Homemade Requesón
   (page 64)
1 (15-ounce) jar pickled cactus
   strips, or 4 large cactus
   paddles, diced (see pages
   76 and 146) and blanched in
   boiling salted water for 3 to
   5 minutes, until just tender
chopped fresh cilantro
crumbled queso fresco
salsa of choice

1 Heat the lard in a skillet over medium heat. When hot, add the onion wedge and garlic. Fry, turning occasionally, until blistered and deep golden brown.

2 Add the beans and mash roughly, using the bottom of a heatproof cup. You don't want them too pasty and smooth. In Spanish, they call the desired texture *martajada*. Add a little bean broth if they look too dry. Cook until the flavors combine, adding more broth as needed, about 5 minutes. Season with salt. Transfer to a bowl nearby.

3 If you're using masa harina, place in a deep bowl and pour 1 cup of the warm water on top. Knead together for about 5 minutes to form a thick, pliable dough. To check whether the dough is sufficiently moist, break off a small ball and flatten it. If the edges crack, you need more water—up to ½ cup. (The masa should be moister than the average tortilla masa, as it will cook longer than a tortilla and shouldn't dry out.) If using fresh tortilla masa, sprinkle with a few drops of water and knead firmly, adding the water a teaspoon at a time until the masa is very soft and creamy, about 5 minutes. (For fresh masa you will only need perhaps ¼ cup water total.) Grab a piece of masa and cover the rest with a damp dish cloth to keep it hydrated.

4 Roll the masa into a ball just larger than a golf ball, and using your palm, flatten into a disk about ¼ inch thick. (You can also place the ball on a tortilla press, but be careful not to press it too thin.) Fresh masa will be much easier to work with than masa harina, but if you're using the latter, keep working and patting, pressing firmly on the masa ball to form a circular shape.

5 Holding the disk in your palm, add 1 to 2 tablespoons beans or requesón to the center, spreading the filling into a longish rectangle, without hitting the top or bottom edges. The filling amount really depends on how big your disk is—if the filling spills out when you try to close the *tlacoyo*, you have too much.

6 Fold both sides of the *tlacoyo* toward the center to enclose the filling. Press the seams together, pinching them closed with your thumbs. Pinch the seams closed with your thumbs. Set aside on a baking sheet and repeat with the remaining masa and filling.

7 Warm a *comal* or nonstick skillet on medium heat. Place the *tlacoyo* in the pan, without oil, and let cook. Once the sides start to dry slightly, turn it over. If you don't start to see golden-brown freckles, turn up the heat; if you see burned spots, lower the heat. Keep turning at intervals until both sides are freckled and crisp, and the edges have puffed a bit, 10 to 12 minutes in all.

8 Garnish with cactus, cilantro, cheese, salsa and onion. Serve warm.

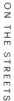

BURRITOS DE FLOR DE CALABAZA
SQUASH FLOWER BURRITOS

Burritos are much more a Northern Mexican snack than a chilango one, but they're gaining in popularity in Mexico City at bars and small cafes. These are not the burritos of the United States. They are smaller—you can hold them with one hand and the filling will not spill out—and they include ingredients like poblano peppers, avocado, steak and cheese. They contain beans but no rice. This recipe is inspired by my favorite street stand in the Zona Rosa, where my go-to order is squash flowers, cheese and beans with Chile Morita Salsa.

1 batch Quick Refried Beans
(see opposite)
1 batch Creamy Chile Morita
Salsa (see opposite)
4 large (12-inch) flour tortillas
2 tablespoons canola oil
1 cup chopped onion
1 cup chopped plum tomatoes,
or any other fresh, ripe tomato
salt
30 squash flowers, stems
removed and torn in half
1 cup shredded Chihuahua
cheese, or any other mild
melting cheese

1   Prepare the refried beans and chile morita salsa, and place in bowls on a clean workspace, next to four dinner plates. Place the tortillas near the stove.

2   Heat 1 tablespoon oil in a large heavy skillet. Working in batches, add half the onion and cook until translucent, 3 to 5 minutes. Add half of the tomatoes and season with salt; cook until the tomatoes have slightly softened, about 4 minutes.

3   Meanwhile, warm 2 flour tortillas on a large griddle or skillet, or in the microwave. Wrap in a cloth to keep warm.

4   Add half of the squash flowers to the pan, plus a little more salt to taste. Stir and cook until the flowers have wilted slightly, about 3 minutes. Separate the mixture into two long, rectangular-shaped piles. Sprinkle ¼ cup cheese onto each pile, covering the filling evenly. Leave undisturbed until the cheese melts, about 1 minute.

5   Place the 2 warm tortillas on plates and smear about 2 tablespoons beans in a rectangular shape that spans the length of each tortilla.

6   Using a spatula, carefully scoop one batch of the cheesy squash-flower filling onto a bean-smeared tortilla. Repeat with the second tortilla.

7   Add about 2 teaspoons of the salsa to each tortilla and fold the tortilla over itself, tuck in the sides, and roll into a burrito.

8   Repeat with the remaining tortillas and filling.

COOKING TIP: *If you can't find squash flowers, try substituting a vegetable mixture that sounds good to you, like corn, mushrooms, and chard.*

QUICK REFRIED BEANS

Refried beans are used in all sorts of Mexican recipes, and not just as a side dish. I like them in Stuffed Cactus Paddles (page 172), Squash Flower Huaraches (page 74), or smeared into a tortilla with a little salsa.

1 teaspoon lard
1 small piece onion (about half of a ½-inch-thick slice)
1 medium garlic clove, peeled
2 cups cooked beans, preferably black or pinto, plus ½ cup cooking liquid, or 1 (20-ounce) can black beans, about half the broth drained
salt

1   Heat a medium skillet to medium-high heat. Add the lard and when hot, add the onion and garlic. Cook until golden and blistered on all sides, about 3 minutes. Add the beans and broth quickly (the liquid may splatter, so don't get too close), and mash with a bean-masher or the bottom of a heatproof cup.

2   Stir and keep mashing until the beans form a semi-chunky paste. If there is too much broth, raise the heat and reduce, stirring often so the beans don't burn. If the beans look too dry, add more broth. Cook until the beans start to congeal and pull easily away from the sides and bottom of the pan, 7 to 10 minutes. Remove from the heat, season with salt if needed, and set aside until ready to use.

CREAMY CHILE MORITA SALSA

This smoky, creamy salsa goes perfectly with the squash flowers. It shouldn't be too hot, though, or else it will overwhelm their delicate flavors. Any leftovers can be stored in an airtight container in the fridge for up to 2 days. You can eat it on fish tacos, with quesadillas, pizza (if you're into that) or anything else that calls for a salsa.

2 medium cloves garlic, unpeeled
5 morita chiles
3 tablespoons mayonnaise, thinned with 1 tablespoon milk and mixed with a squirt of fresh lime juice
salt

1   Heat a *comal* or nonstick skillet to medium and add the garlic at the outer edges, away from direct heat, so they don't burn. Cook until blackened in spots and slightly squishy, 5 to 7 minutes.

2   Lightly toast the morita chiles on both sides until they release their aroma, 30 to 60 seconds per side. Transfer to a bowl of hot water and let sit for 15 to 20 minutes, or until the skins soften.

3   Remove the chile stems and slice three of the chiles open to remove the seeds. Place all the chiles in a blender jar with the lime-accented mayonnaise, ½ cup plus 2 tablespoons water and ½ teaspoon salt. Blend until smooth. If the salsa is too hot, add more mayonnaise and water. Transfer to a bowl and set aside or refrigerate until ready to use.

TACOS DE CANASTA
STEAMED TACOS

Bike-riding vendors sell these tacos across the city from little baskets that sit above their back wheels. Fished out warm from a nest of paper and cloth, the taco is supremely satisfying—a soft, greasy half-moon filled with refried beans, or mashed and fried potato. In other areas of Mexico they're known as tacos al vapor or tacos sudados.

This dish is not the easiest to make at home, but if you've got a basket, it's a fun activity to do with friends and makes great party food. (I highly recommend making these with friends; it's a lot of work for one person.) You'll need to line the basket with a large cloth, then a layer of sturdy plastic such as grocery bags or a painting drop cloth, and finally, a layer of parchment, butcher paper, or newspaper. Only the paper should directly touch the food.

For the potato filling:

2 pounds Yukon Gold potatoes, rinsed and peeled
2 tablespoons lard
½ medium onion, cut into 2-inch slivers
2 medium cloves garlic, peeled and minced
1 teaspoon salt

For the bean filling:

1 tablespoon plus 1 teaspoon lard
⅛ medium white onion, chopped
1 garlic clove, peeled
1 (16-ounce) package dried beans, such as pinto or black, cooked until soft, plus 1 cup of reserved bean broth, or 2 (15.5-ounce) cans black or pinto beans, liquid reserved
1 teaspoon salt, or more to taste

For the tacos:

5 ounces lard (see Tip)
40 corn tortillas (see Tip)
Pickled Onions and Habanero (page 29)
Raw Tomatillo Salsa (page 26)
Árbol Chile and Peanut Salsa (page 29)

1 To make the potato filling, place the potatoes in a large saucepan and cover with 2 inches cold water. Bring to a boil, and then lower the heat to medium and cover the pan halfway. Simmer until very tender and the outer flesh sloughs off slightly, about 45 minutes. Remove the potatoes from the water to cool, reserving ½ cup of the potato water. Once cooled to room temperature, mash the potatoes into a smooth purée with your hands, a potato ricer or a food mill. Set aside.

2 Heat the lard in a large skillet over medium heat. When hot, add the onion and cook, stirring constantly, until translucent, 2 to 3 minutes. Add the garlic and cook until aromatic. Stir in the potatoes, reserved potato water, and salt. Once warmed through, remove from the heat and cover to keep warm.

3 To make the bean filling, heat the lard in a large skillet over medium-high heat. When hot, add the onion and garlic—they should sizzle when they hit the pan—and fry until golden and blistered on all sides, 3 to 5 minutes. Add the beans and broth quickly as they may splatter. Stir in the salt and lower the heat to medium-low. Mash the beans with a bean masher or the underside of a heatproof cup, until you have a textured paste. Cook until most of the liquid has been absorbed. If the beans look too dry, add more broth. (The ideal texture should be creamy and soft and perhaps the slightest bit runny.) Season with more salt, if needed. Remove the pan from the heat and set aside. Reserve extra cooking liquid as the beans may dry out the longer they sit.

4 For the tacos, melt 3 ounces lard in a small saucepan, and keep warm on very low heat. Nearby, assemble a work station with a pastry brush, the potatoes, beans, and lined basket.

5 Warm the tortillas two or three at a time on a *comal* or nonstick skillet heated to medium until soft and pliable. Don't overheat or they will be too crispy to fold. Keep warm in a dishcloth or tortilla warmer.

6   Place 2 to 3 tablespoons filling on one half of a tortilla. Fold and brush with warm melted lard and pat down slightly so the taco lays flat. Place in the basket, the edges of each taco overlapping slightly. Repeat until you have an even layer, brush with lard again, then stack another layer on top, brushing each layer with more lard. (It's helpful to assign one filling to a specific side of the basket, so you know what you're getting when you reach in later.)

7   Once all the tacos have been prepared, heat the remaining 2 ounces lard over high heat. When smoking, after about a minute, quickly pour on top of the tacos. They should sizzle. Wrap tightly with the layers of paper, plastic and cloth. The tacos will keep warm for at least 3 hours. Serve with the salsas.

COOKING TIP: *Don't skimp on the fat. Lard is the most flavorful, although vegetable oil will work in a pinch. Both must be heated to smoking before the basket is closed or else the tacos will not stay warm. Also, make sure the potatoes are well cooked—you want as smooth a texture as possible.*

Because this dish is so simple, it really matters that you use the best tortillas you can find, ideally ones made from fresh nixtamalized masa. Any leftovers crisp up nicely on the comal.

TORTAS DE PAVO
TURKEY TORTAS WITH CHIPOTLE SALSA

Turkey tortas—sandwiches stacked with oven-baked or slow-fried turkey—are immensely popular in the Downtown Historic Center, and elsewhere around Mexico City. It's not surprising given the turkey's long history in Mexico: The animal was first domesticated there, several hundred years before the Spaniards arrived.

My favorite stand sits not too far from the famed San Juan Market. The owner, Luis Buenrostro Gutiérrez, has sold his sandwich in the same way for more than forty years. Turkey simmers for hours in a large cauldron of lard, and then chunks are sliced off, grilled and placed on an open-faced telera roll smeared with ripe avocado. Vinegary, tart chipotle salsa and a few leaves of pungent, peppery pápaloquelite, a native Mexican herb, finish it off. He gave me this recipe with the strict instructions that readers only use lard—"It must be lard, no ifs, ands, or buts!"—and that they do not substitute refried beans for avocado. (He actually looked disgusted at that idea. Even the young guy stacking soda bottles looked at me askance.) These are surprisingly easy to make at home, assuming you can find enough lard.

6 pounds lard

4 pounds turkey legs

salt

1 (7-ounce) can chipotles en adobo

1 medium jalapeño, chopped roughly, with seeds

2½ tablespoons apple cider vinegar

canola oil

4 to 6 *telera* rolls (see Tip)

1 large Haas avocado

1 bunch pápaloquelite, leaves only, optional

COOKING TIPS: *If you can't find telera, the flat roll traditionally used for tortas in Mexico, try substituting a buttery hamburger bun. If you can't find pápalo, which is sold at some Latino grocery stores, leave it out.*

Strive for the most even heat possible when cooking the turkey. The lard should bubble gently—the flame shouldn't be so low that it does not bubble at all.

1 Melt the lard over low heat in a large stockpot. Add the turkey legs so they're submerged in the fat and raise the flame to high. Don't disturb them until the lard starts to boil and foam, about 10 minutes.

2 Using tongs, carefully turn the legs in the lard and turn the heat to low. Cook for 1 hour, undisturbed, and then sprinkle ¾ teaspoon salt into the pot. Do not stir.

3 Carefully turn the legs, making sure they're submerged in the lard again, and cook for another 45 minutes. Turn the legs again and cook about 1 hour more, for a total of 2 hours and 45 minutes, or until very tender.

4 Clutching the bone-end with tongs (trying to lift them out by the meaty end will cause the leg to fall apart), place the turkey legs on a rimmed baking sheet lined with a wire rack and cool to room temperature, about 45 minutes. At this point you can store the meat in an airtight container for up to a week. Strain the lard, let it cool, and refrigerate for future use.

5 To prepare the salsa, place the chipotles en adobo, jalapeño, vinegar, 2 teaspoons water and ½ teaspoon salt in a blender and pulse until thick and chunky. Remove to a small bowl and set aside.

6 Grease a *comal* or nonstick skillet lightly with the oil and heat to medium. Cut open the rolls and toast, about 1 minute per side. Scrape off any crumbs from the grill and place the rolls on a workspace. Slather one-quarter of the avocado on one side like a paste, and top with 2 teaspoons salsa and a sprinkle of pápalo leaves, if using.

7 Cut the turkey legs into small pieces against the grain, and then place the meat in the heated skillet to crisp lightly, 30 to 60 seconds. Transfer to the empty pieces of bread, placing the avocado-laden bread on top to close. Cut in half and serve immediately.

TACOS AL PASTOR
MARINATED, SPIT-ROASTED TACOS

Tacos al pastor—*made from marinated pork that's been roasted on a vertical spit—are wildly popular in Mexico City, particularly at night. The best* taqueros *put on a show, slicing off bits of caramelized meat and catching it in one hand (or behind their back!), and then reaching above the meat to slice off a piece of warm, juicy pineapple. According to city folklore, these tacos were invented in the capital. The dish is a direct descendant of shawarma, brought by Lebanese immigrants who arrived in Mexico in the early twentieth century.*

The marinade in this recipe comes from Tacos Don Guero in the Cuauhtémoc neighborhood, whose taqueros *were kind enough to explain their ingredients to me at six a.m. one weekday morning. Obviously very few people at home will have a vertical spit—part of what gives* tacos al pastor *its signature flavor—but a grill would work well, or a blazing-hot cast iron skillet or griddle greased with a little lard.*

1　The day before you plan to eat, place the pork in a large bowl and toss with the lime juice and salt. Heat a *comal* or nonstick skillet to medium-high heat. Add the onion wedge and garlic, placing the garlic near the edge, away from direct heat. Cook until soft and blackened in spots, turning occasionally, about 7 minutes. Peel the garlic and place both items in a blender jar. Crumble the achiote paste into the blender and add the vinegar, cumin seed, peanuts and bay leaf along with the cinnamon stick, cloves and allspice. Blend until smooth. Pour the marinade over the meat and toss to coat. Cover with plastic wrap and refrigerate for 24 hours.

2　The next day, prepare the garnishes: Chop the pineapple, slice the limes into wedges, prepare the salsa, and chop the cilantro and onion.

3　Heat a large heavy skillet to high heat and add 1 teaspoon lard. When smoking, add one piece of marinated steak. The meat should sizzle and smoke, so make sure you have a working fan and vent on your stove. Cook until the meat starts to release its juices and lighten slightly in color, 2 to 3 minutes, then flip and cook 2 to 3 minutes more. Both sides should have dark-brown charred spots; if they don't, raise the heat higher. Transfer to a cutting board and repeat with the remaining steaks, scraping the pan well to remove any burned bits between frying.

4　Scrape out the pan once more and cook the pineapple until soft and charred in spots. Remove to a bowl.

5　Warm the corn tortillas on a *comal* or nonstick skillet and place in a dishcloth to keep warm. Chop the meat into small pieces. Serve on a platter and let guests feed themselves, passing the tortillas and garnishes.

2 pounds pork butt roast, sliced into
　very thin steaks
¼ cup fresh lime juice
¾ teaspoon salt
¼ medium onion, plus 1 cup chopped
2 large cloves garlic, unpeeled
½ bar achiote paste
¼ cup plus 1 tablespoon apple cider vinegar
½ heaping teaspoon whole cumin seed,
　toasted
2 tablespoons raw unsalted peanuts, toasted
1 small fresh Mexican bay leaf
1 (2-inch) cinnamon stick
2 cloves
2 allspice berries
2 cups chopped fresh pineapple
5 limes, cut into wedges
salsa of choice
1 cup chopped fresh cilantro
1 cup chopped onion
lard or vegetable oil
24 corn tortillas

ENCHILADAS VERDES
GREEN CHICKEN ENCHILADAS

Typical Mexican enchiladas arrive rolled up and stuffed, but at my favorite enchilada street stand—the inspiration for this recipe—they're stacked in a messy, luxurious pile, with separate individual layers of corn tortillas, fresh cilantro and onion, green enchilada sauce, shredded cheese and chicken. The whole thing is topped with a blanket of crema and more cheese. It's almost like a deconstructed lasagna. The dish is enough to make you fall deeply in love with Mexico City—particularly when the corn tortillas are homemade, and the green sauce is prepared with a slow-simmering pot of fresh chicken stock.

3 pounds skinless chicken legs, thighs, and breasts, fat trimmed

1 pound chicken backs, fat trimmed

3 medium cloves garlic, unpeeled

1 dried Mexican bay leaf

5 peppercorns

1 medium onion, quartered

1¾ teaspoons salt

¼ teaspoon freshly ground black pepper

2 pounds tomatillos, husked and rinsed

2 large serrano chiles

1 tablespoon plus 2 teaspoons lard or canola oil

24 corn tortillas

½ cup chopped fresh cilantro

2 cups Homemade Crema (page 139)

1 cup mild, shredded cheese, such as Monterrey Jack or Colby

1 At least 2 hours before you'd like to eat, place the chicken, 1 garlic clove, the bay leaf, peppercorns and a quarter of the onion in a large stockpot. Cover with cold water and bring to a boil. Lower the heat to very low, cover and simmer for 25 minutes. Remove the chicken legs, thighs and breasts with tongs or a slotted spoon and let cool. Discard the chicken backs and strain the stock; set aside.

2 Once cool enough to handle, shred the meat and season with ¾ teaspoon salt and the black pepper. Set aside.

3 Place the tomatillos in a large saucepan. Add the remaining 2 cloves garlic, peeled, and 2 quarters of the onion. Cover with cold water. Bring to a boil, then simmer on medium heat until the tomatillos turn pea green and soften, about 12 minutes. Transfer to a bowl and let cool. (Vegetarians can reserve the cooking water, turn up the flame, and reduce for 15 to 20 minutes, to use in lieu of chicken stock, if they choose.)

4 Stem the chiles and chop roughly with the cooked garlic. Add to a blender jar with half of the tomatillo mixture, and ½ cup of the strained chicken stock. (If you have a high-powered blender, toss all the ingredients in at once.) Blend until smooth. Add the remaining tomatillo-onion mixture and 1 teaspoon salt, and blend again until smooth.

5 Warm 1 tablespoon lard in a large skillet over medium heat. When hot, add the sauce in one quick pour, being careful as it might splatter. Cook until the flavors meld, about 5 minutes.

6 Heat 2 teaspoons lard in a small skillet over medium heat and swirl to coat the bottom. Fry the tortillas lightly, one at a time, until slightly tougher but still pliable, about 30 seconds per side. (They shouldn't be crisp.) As you work, remove the fried tortillas to serving plates—I like to serve 4 tortillas per person. Fold the tortillas in a half-moon shape and make sure they sit in an even layer on each plate.

7   Dice the remaining quarter of onion. Ladle ¾ cup sauce over over each serving of tortillas, spreading slightly so the tortillas are entirely smothered in sauce. Add a layer of diced onion and cilantro, a layer of shredded cheese, a layer of chicken, some crema and another layer of sauce. Top with another light sprinkling of diced onion.

COOKING TIP: *I recommend making your own light stock here, using the water in which you've cooked the chicken; see recipe on page 98. If you can find a hen, which Mexican cooks consider to be the most flavorful stock base, use that. If you're vegetarian, this dish can still be pretty wonderful, especially if you use homemade vegetable stock.*

ESQUITES
STREET CORN IN A CUP

1 (14-ounce) package *mote* (preferably Goya),
    or 2 (16-ounce) packages frozen sweet
    corn (see Tip)
2 tablespoons canola oil
½ medium onion, chopped
2 medium cloves garlic, minced
12 to 15 stems epazote, or less if very
    pungent
1 dried árbol chile, toasted, stemmed
    and seeded
2 teaspoons salt
2 large limes, cut in half
chile piquín powder, such as Tajín brand
mayonnaise, optional
good-quality crumbled aged-cheese, such
    as *queso añejo*, ricotta salata or Romano,
    optional

Chilango *street corn vendors come out at dusk only, and they sell two snacks:* elote—*a big, starchy ear of corn, crusted with mayonnaise, slightly funky* añejo *cheese and chile powder—and* esquites, *a mix of corn stewed with epazote and spices, and served in a cup with mayo, lime juice and chile powder. The latter is my favorite, particularly for its dense, hearty Mexican corn kernels, which taste nothing like sweet American corn. To recreate that corn's same chewy heft when I'm not in Mexico, I use* mote, *a dried lightly nixtamalized Andean corn. It cooks for at least an hour, so the broth has more time to develop flavor. The result is so warm and comforting, I think it works on its own as a main dish.*

1   If using *mote*, the night before, place it in a large pot and cover with cold water. Let soak overnight. The next day, drain and cover with 3 inches of fresh water, and bring to boil. Lower the flame, and once the cooking surface is only gently bubbling, cover and simmer on low for 30 minutes. Drain and reserve the cooking liquid.

2   Heat the oil in a heavy pot over medium-low heat. Add the onion and garlic and cook until the onion is translucent, about 3 minutes. If using *mote*, add to the pot with 5 cups of the reserved cooking liquid, or a mixture of cooking liquid and water. If using frozen corn, add to the pot with 4 cups water. Add the epazote and dried chile, raise the heat and bring to a boil. Stir in the salt, lower the heat, and simmer until the corn is tender—for *mote*, 30 to 35 minutes, or until the kernel is translucent when cut in half. For frozen corn, this takes about 10 minutes.

3   To serve, fill a standard-size mug or shallow bowl halfway with corn. Spritz lime juice on top, and cover with more corn. Top with more lime juice, chile powder, plus mayonnaise and cheese if desired. Serve immediately.

COOKING TIPS: *You can find mote at Latin grocery stores or online. If it's not available, dried, nixtamalized pozole corn would work (this generally has a smaller kernel than* mote*), or fresh or frozen sweet corn as a last option. Skip the mayo if you like, but the lime juice here is essential.*

GORDITAS DE NATA
SWEET CREAM BISCUITS

You can find these tiny, golden-brown biscuits near the Basilica de Guadalupe, Mexico's oldest and most famous religious site. They're hard to ignore: vendors cry out for you to try a sample, and an enticing yellow-cake smell wafts around them at all times. Similar versions are sold in other parts of Mexico, including Michoacán.

The main ingredient is nata, or clotted cream. Dense and rich—and still small enough to fit in the palm of your hand—these biscuits are unbeatable in the morning with coffee, or as a sweet side to something like Mexican-style Eggs (page 86).

1   In a medium bowl, whisk together the flour, baking powder, baking soda and salt. Set aside.

2   In a large bowl, stir together the clotted cream, sugar and vanilla.

3   Add the flour mixture, a little at a time, to the clotted cream, stirring with a rubber spatula and then kneading with your hands until a cohesive dough forms. Add the milk if the mixture looks too dry.

4   Divide the dough in half and transfer one half to a floured surface. Roll out to ¼ inch thick. Cut into small rounds using a 2-inch biscuit cutter. Cook on an ungreased *comal* or nonstick skillet heated to low, flipping occasionally, until golden brown and crisp on both sides, and no longer doughy at the edges, about 5 minutes.

5   Serve warm with butter if desired, or any leftover clotted cream substitute. Reheat any leftover *gorditas* on the stovetop.

2 cups all-purpose flour
1 teaspoon baking powder
½ teaspoon baking soda
¼ teaspoon salt
1 (6-ounce) jar clotted cream, or 6 ounces Clotted Cream Substitute (recipe follows)
¼ cup sugar
½ teaspoon vanilla extract
1 to 2 tablespoons milk, or more if necessary

COOKING TIP: *These cook on the stovetop, so make sure the heat is very low and that they're not rolled out too thin. The ideal texture is soft and chewy.*

English grocery stores sell clotted cream or you can find it online. My recipe for a clotted cream substitute is below, just in case you have trouble tracking it down.

CLOTTED CREAM SUBSTITUTE

Whip the heavy cream until soft peaks form. Fold in the sour cream and sugar. Use immediately, or place in a strainer or sieve set over a bowl, and store in the fridge for up to 3 days.

1 cup heavy cream
⅓ cup sour cream
1 tablespoon confectioners' sugar

CHAMPURRADO
THICKENED MEXICAN HOT CHOCOLATE

This is a thicker, more decadent version of the warm chocolate-flavored beverage that's sold on the streets to accompany tamales. You can find versions of it all around Mexico, but the base tends to have some sort of combination of chocolate, corn (either masa or a toasted ground corn called pinole) and sugar. My version is so rich that I think it works as dessert. (Or, if you are me, a 3 p.m. snack.) The masa flavor isn't extremely noticeable, so if you'd like more of a corn boost, add more masa or stir in some pinole, which can be found at select Mexican grocery stores.

1   If using masa harina, add ¾ cup warm water to a small bowl and sprinkle in the masa a little bit at a time, whisking after each addition until it forms a thick batter. If using fresh masa, add ½ cup water to a blender jar and crumble the masa into small pieces. Blend on low into a thick paste. Strain the fresh masa paste into another bowl, pushing on the bottom of the strainer with a spatula.

2   For the masa harina version, bring 1¼ cups water and the cinnamon stick, if using, to a boil in a medium saucepan. (For fresh masa, use 2 cups water.) Add the masa batter and immediately whisk until dissolved. Lower the flame to medium or medium-low and cook until thick and very bubbly, 3 to 5 minutes.

3   Over medium heat, add the milk, chocolate, sugar and salt. Simmer, stirring constantly and scraping the bottom of the pan, until it thickens more deeply, 15 to 20 minutes.

4   Discard the cinnamon stick, if using, and serve warm, ladled into mugs. To reheat, add more milk to thin out, and warm on the stovetop at a low temperature.

½ cup plus 2 tablespoons masa harina, or 4 ounces fresh tortilla masa

1 (3-inch) cinnamon stick, optional

3 cups whole milk

5½ ounces good-quality Mexican chocolate (about 2 tablets)

1 tablespoon sugar

1 pinch salt

COOKING TIP: *Using good-quality Mexican chocolate matters. Rancho Gordo sells an excellent variety, as well as Taza, Hernán and Susana Trilling's Season of My Heart brand. The quantity of cinnamon varies in each chocolate, so taste a small piece first and then decide whether you'd like to add the cinnamon stick.*

CHAPTER 2

IN THE MARKETS

In Mexico City, there are two types of markets: *mercados*, generally boxy buildings full of produce stalls and eateries, and *tianguis* (tee-AHN-geese), outdoor markets that move to different neighborhoods throughout the week. Many *mercado* buildings in Mexico City were constructed in the middle of the twentieth century, and there's a sense, stepping inside, that things haven't changed much.

Vendors own their stalls and treat them like small pieces of real estate. They sell neatly arranged piles of tropical fruits, shaggy heads of purple-tinged and curly leaf lettuce, tangles of cilantro, sacks of dried beans in various colors. Some stands specialize in herbal remedies and teas (a vestige of Mexico's indigenous past), and the bushy herbs are stacked so high that you can barely see the vendor's face. Other stands sell paper plates and styrofoam cups, or cat, dog and bird food.

At the butcher counters, bright yellow chickens lie in neat rows, open-air, on the countertops. Steak and pork vendors have refrigerated cases, but they leave items out to lure in customers: large, crinkled sheets of *chicharrón* (pork crackling) and reddish wedges of oily *chicharrón prensado*, a type of terrine made from leftover pig parts. The lard, white and whipped and sold by the kilo, always reminds me of cake frosting.

MERCADOS VS. TIANGUIS

The *mercado* is as much about eating as it is shopping. Every market offers prepared food, sold either at lunch counters or small restaurants, and all of it is cooked daily or à la minute. You can find fresh juices and tortas, *guisados* and tacos, and pitchers of *agua frescas*. Eating there, your market bags resting at your feet, the strum of a guitar or some other music in your ear from a wandering musician—it's hard not to romanticize the experience, particularly when you've spent your life shopping at bland supermarkets.

The *tianguis*, from the Nahuatl word "tianquitzli," meaning plaza or market, is an open-air market that usually spans several blocks, with stands offering fresh produce, prepared food, clothes, shoes and other odds and ends. The vibe is wilder than the *mercado*—vendors don't hesitate to yell out their wares at passers by. "Limón limón limón limón!" Limes limes limes limes! "Papaya papaya papayaaaaa!" There are ambulant vendors too: men toting big glass jars of honey and pollen, flat baskets of fresh herbs, coolers of homemade tamales, fresh cheeses or stacks of wooden hangers.

It's interesting to ponder how long all of this will go on, as Mexican demographics have changed. More women now work outside the home and families report having less time to cook. The *mercados* and *tianguis* are only open during business hours, so they don't fit the average working person's schedule. Some *mercados* have lost most of their tenants, leaving huge, half-empty shells in otherwise bustling residential neighborhoods.

I don't take my market experience for granted. One of my favorite ways to spend an afternoon is at my local *mercado* in the Roma neighborhood, greeting the vendors who know my face and asking for recipes for ingredients I've never seen before. Every single vendor I have ever asked for a recipe has given me one. Their instructions almost always start with, "Sofríe su ajito, cebollita, y chilito para darle sabor..." (You fry garlic, onion and a little chile to give it flavor...) With the vendors' help, the recipes that follow reflect the snacks, tacos and prepared dishes found at markets I've loved.

CAFÉ DE OLLA
SWEET CINNAMON-SPIKED COFFEE

Café de olla—literally, "coffee from the pot"—is typically served for breakfast at markets across the city and across Mexico, comprising coffee that's been mixed with piloncillo, *a type of unrefined Mexican cane sugar, and cinnamon. The beverage is traditionally brewed in a clay pot. I'm not generally a fan of sweetened coffee, but this drink pairs perfectly with heavy, spicy Mexican breakfasts. The* piloncillo *is warm and molasses-y, and cinnamon and cloves add a bit more depth of flavor than you'd find in regular coffee.*

1 Pour 6 cups water into a large stainless steel saucepan or clay pot, and then add the *piloncillo*, cinnamon stick and cloves. Heat on high and cook until the *piloncillo* completely dissolves. Bring the mixture to a boil, add the ground coffee and bring to another boil.

2 Lower the flame to medium and simmer for about 3 minutes. Turn off the heat, cover the pot and let the grounds settle to the bottom, 10 to 15 minutes.

3 Strain the coffee using a fine-mesh strainer or cheesecloth. Discard the coffee grounds, cinnamon stick and cloves. Serve warm, ladling into individual mugs.

¼ cup plus 2 tablespoons chopped or grated *piloncillo,* or dark brown sugar

1 cinnamon stick

4 cloves

6 tablespoons medium or dark roast coffee, ground

COOKING TIP: *In Mexico City,* piloncillo *is sold in small, unwrapped cones or in small nuggets. In other parts of Mexico, the sugar may come in blocks or circular disks called* panela *or* panocha. *In the U.S., you can usually find* piloncillo *at Latin grocery stores, but you can substitute brown sugar in a pinch.*

This is not an overly strong coffee, and it's always served plain, without milk. But if you want it weaker, add more water. Leftovers can be stored in the refrigerator for up to two days. It's delicious hot or cold.

HOW TO GRATE OR CHOP PILONCILLO

A sharp knife works best to cut piloncillo. *To do so, turn the cone upside down and grab it by the wider end. Tilt it at a 45-degree angle, and using your knife, cut the* piloncillo *at the narrower end, slicing through at a slight angle. The pieces should slice off more or less cleanly. If the* piloncillo *is very hard, keep clutching the* piloncillo *by the wider end, and use your knife to flake off small bits. Do not put the* piloncillo *in your food processor, or you might break the machine.*

LICUADO DE MAMEY
MAMEY MILKSHAKE

Mamey, pronounced "mah-MAY," was the first Mexican tropical fruit to completely bewitch me. The football-shaped fruit has a creamy, sunset-colored flesh, and tastes like a mix of pumpkins and cherries. Most chilangos eat mamey raw or blend it with milk to make a thick shake called a licuado. At local markets, licuado stands carry a selection of grains, herbs and nuts, and they'll make any combination the customer wants. I include my preference below for puffed amaranth and raw oats, which add a nuttiness to mamey's sweet flavor.

3 cups whole milk

2 cups chopped fresh mamey, or 1 (14-ounce package) frozen mamey pulp, thawed

¼ cup raw rolled oats (not steel-cut)

2 tablespoons puffed amaranth

1 tablespoon honey or other desired sweetener, optional

Place the milk, mamey, oats, and amaranth in a blender jar, and blend on high until smooth. Add more mamey if desired, or honey. (Fresh mamey may not need any sweetener.) Pour into two glasses—or one if you're especially hungry—and serve immediately.

COOKING TIP: *Latin grocery stores or Mexican markets stock frozen mamey pulp, while health food stores generally carry puffed amaranth (for instructions on how to puff your own, see page 163). Some Mexican grocery stores in larger urban areas may also stock fresh mamey seasonally. If you can't find mamey, don't substitute anything else, as the flavor won't be the same.*

TEPACHE
SWEETENED FERMENTED PINEAPPLE JUICE

On a hot, early spring Mexico City day, before the summer rains arrive to clean the air and cool everything down, there's nothing better than an icy glass of tepache, or sweet, fermented pineapple juice. It's sold at markets and street stands across the city, sometimes in little plastic baggies wrapped around a straw. The taste is sweet and floral and slightly funky, almost like a very mild fruit beer. (The alcohol level here is minimal.) This makes a great party punch, or a refreshing drink on a hot day.

1   About 3 days before you wish to drink the *tepache*, wash the pineapple well and cut it into pieces, keeping the rind on. Place the pineapple in a large pot with 1 gallon of water and the cloves, allspice, and cinnamon stick. Leave it for 2 days, covered loosely with a double layer of cheesecloth. (Feel free to peek at the *tepache* while it sits; it won't hurt the drink.) On the second day, you should start to smell some pineapple funk emitting from the pot.

2   Place the *piloncillo* cones in a small saucepan and pour 1 cup water over them. Cook on low heat, stirring often, until the cones dissolve completely. Remove from the heat and let cool about 30 minutes. Stir the cooled *piloncillo* syrup into the pineapple, along with the beer. Cover and let sit for another day.

3   On the last day, you may notice some white mold spots on the liquid's surface. That's okay. Ignore them. Strain the liquid into a large serving container, and discard the pineapple chunks and spices. Stir and serve over ice.

COOKING TIP: *To ferment the pineapple, you need a large (10-quart) pot and some cheesecloth. The drink needs to interact with the air in order for it to start fermenting—don't cover it tightly with a lid. If you like sweeter drinks, add more sugar. For a more fermented taste, let the pot sit out longer than three days. The drink will keep in an airtight container in the refrigerator for up to five days, but warning: it may get boozier as it sits.*

1 very ripe, soft pineapple, about 3 to 4 pounds
2 cloves
2 allspice berries
1 (3-inch) cinnamon stick
2 (7-ounce) cones of *piloncillo* or light brown sugar
1 (12-ounce) bottle light or lager-style beer, such as Modelo Especial

REQUESÓN
HOMEMADE REQUESÓN CHEESE

Requesón is a salty, spreadable cheese sold at markets around the city. It tastes like a creamier, more acidic version of ricotta. Making it from scratch is easy: You curdle milk with vinegar or another acid such as lime juice, and then warm it and watch the curds form. Most street vendors use it as a tlacoyo filling but you can use requesón for all sorts of things—stirred into scrambled eggs and tomatoes, smeared into a corn tortilla with salsa or, less authentically Mexican, spread onto a piece of toast with honey or mixed in a dip of fresh herbs and olive oil.

1 gallon whole milk
½ cup white vinegar
1 teaspoon salt

1 Stir together the milk and vinegar in a large heavy-bottomed pot. Cook over medium-high heat until large, thick curds form on the milk's surface and the curds have clearly separated from the thinner, clearer whey, 35 to 40 minutes if using cold milk directly from the fridge, or slightly less if using room-temperature milk. The curds won't necessarily look big and lumpy—think more of a layer of algae on a lake. Try not to disturb the milk too much while it cooks, in order to give the curds more time to come together.

2 Remove the pan from the heat and let sit, uncovered, for 10 minutes, to allow the curds to continue to thicken.

3 Line a fine-mesh strainer with a layer of cheesecloth and set over a bowl. Using a slotted spoon, transfer the curds to the cheesecloth and let sit for 45 minutes to 1 hour, or until room temperature. (This gives the cheese time to set and cool off.)

4 Transfer the cheese to a bowl or airtight container. Stir in the salt, mixing until thoroughly combined. Use immediately, or chill first in the refrigerator.

COOKING TIP: *Homogenized, pasteurized milk works fine here, but make sure the milk is not ultra-homogenized or else the curds may not come together. This recipe also divides and multiplies easily. Leftovers can be stored in an airtight container in the refrigerator for up to three days.*

POZOLE BLANCO
WHITE POZOLE

Several varieties of pozole, *a pork and hominy stew, exist all over Mexico, but only in the capital can you find so many of them in one place, from green pumpkin-seed-thickened* pozole *from Guerrero to spicy red* pozole *from Jalisco. Mexico City's markets and* fondas *sell large, steaming bowls, accompanied by the typical garnishes: radishes, Mexican oregano, chopped onion, chile powder, tostadas. My favorite is the simple, restorative* pozole blanco. *I start by cooking pork ribs, shoulder and pigs' feet for a few hours in an aromatic broth, then stew hominy in the same broth until the kernels burst open. The result is a rich, satisfying soup, elevated further by contrasting accompaniments.* Pozole *reheats beautifully and you can store leftovers in the freezer.*

1   The night before you wish to eat, place the hominy in a large pot, cover with cold water and soak overnight.

2   The next day, rinse the pigs' feet well and place in a large bowl. Cover with cold water and let sit for 1 hour. (Opinions vary on whether soaking pigs' feet is necessary; I'm doing it here, because that's the way I learned to prepare them.)

3   Rinse the pigs' feet and place them in a large deep pot along with the pork shoulder, ribs, onion wedge and garlic. Cover with cold water and bring to a boil. Skim off any scum that floats to the surface. Lower the heat to medium and simmer until the meat is tender, about 2½ hours, adding more water when the liquid evaporates and the meat is no longer submerged.

4   Remove the meat from the pot, reserving the pot and liquid, and let cool, then shred or cut into small pieces; set aside. (Note: the pigs' feet will not have much meat, but they help add a gelatinous quality to the broth.)

5   Drain the hominy and discard the soaking water. Add the kernels to the pot containing the meat broth. Bring to a boil and cook, stirring occasionally, until the kernels just begin to split apart into a flower-like shape, 60 to 90 minutes. The kernels may not flower evenly, which is okay.

6   Return the meat to the pot and stir in the salt, tasting for more if needed. Cook on medium heat for 10 to 15 minutes, until the flavors meld.

7   Serve warm in large deep bowls, accompanied by all the garnishes: tostadas, to be slathered in a layer of crema; a plate of shredded lettuce or cabbage; and small bowls of chopped onion, sliced radishes, *chicharrón*, if using, Mexican oregano and chile powder. Pass lime wedges and salsa at the table.

COOKING TIPS: *In the U.S., you can buy pozole corn that has already been nixtamalized and dried (Rancho Gordo and Anson Mills sell great varieties), which saves some time. Don't buy canned hominy, which is mushy and lacks flavor. One acceptable substitution would be* mote *corn, which is also pre-nixtamalized and only requires soaking overnight. You can find pigs' feet at most Mexican or Asian grocers.*

1 (16-ounce) package dried, nixtamalized hominy

2 pigs' feet, weighing about 2½ to 3 pounds

1 pound pork shoulder, left whole

1 pound pork ribs

½ medium white onion, plus 1½ cups chopped

2 cloves garlic, peeled

1 tablespoon salt, or more to taste

24 tostadas

2 cups Homemade Crema (page 139)

½ head of iceberg lettuce or cabbage, shredded

1 small bunch radishes, sliced

chicharrón (pork cracklings), broken into pieces, optional (page 136)

2 tablespoons Mexican oregano

1 tablespoon toasted and ground dried árbol chile, or ground chile piquín

5 limes, quartered

hot, vinegary salsa such as Valentina or Cholula

CÓCTEL DE CAMARÓN CON PULPO
SHRIMP AND OCTOPUS COCKTAIL

Sweet and slightly tangy, the Mexican version of shrimp cocktail is nothing like the New England version. It's softer, lighter—something you can tuck into with a beer while still leaving room for a few tacos. In Mexico City, these citrusy, tomato-based cocktails can be found at market stalls and street stands, inspired by versions sold on Mexico's Gulf Coast. They are often eaten as appetizers, or as a complement to another heavier fried dish. The base of the sauce is generally ketchup, thinned out with a little citrus and either broth or mineral water. The dish is always garnished with avocado, which marries perfectly with the ketchup.

salt

1 pound fresh octopus, cleaned and cut into 1-inch pieces

⅛ medium onion, plus ½ cup chopped

1 dried Mexican bay leaf

1 pound fresh shrimp, rinsed, peeled, and cleaned

¾ cup ketchup

3 tablespoons fresh lime juice, plus 2 limes cut into quarters

½ cup roughly chopped fresh cilantro

1 ripe Haas avocado, peeled, pitted, and sliced

12 tostadas, or 24 saltine crackers

hot, vinegary salsa such as Valentina or Cholula

1 Fill a medium saucepan two-thirds full with water. Bring to a strong boil and add 1 teaspoon salt. When the salt dissolves, add the fresh octopus. Lower the flame to medium-low and simmer for about 45 minutes, partially covered, stirring occasionally, until tender. Remove the octopus from the water and drain or freeze the broth for another use. Set the octopus aside to cool, then refrigerate once it has reached room temperature.

2 Rinse out the saucepan and fill again two-thirds full with water. Add the onion wedge and bay leaf, and bring to a vigorous boil. Add a hefty pinch of salt, then add the shrimp and cook until just tender and pink, 1 to 2 minutes. Transfer the shrimp to a bowl and strain and reserve ¾ cup broth. Cool the shrimp slightly, toss with a little salt, and then refrigerate. Cool the broth before using. (To speed things up, you can pour the broth into a measuring cup and set in an ice water bath.)

3 In a medium bowl, whisk together the ketchup, reserved broth, lime juice and ¼ teaspoon salt.

4 Spoon the shrimp and octopus into tall cocktail glasses or shallow bowls. Top each serving with about ¼ cup sauce—enough to coat the seafood—and garnish with a small handful of chopped cilantro and onion, and 2 or 3 thin slices of avocado.

5 Serve immediately with tostadas or saltines, passing the lime wedges and hot sauce at the table.

COOKING TIPS: *The cocktail sauce should be thin but not soupy, and the ratios can be tweaked to your personal taste. Drizzling on vinegary hot sauce adds a nice kick, and fresh, diced tomatoes add sweetness and texture. Using fresh seafood instead of frozen boosts the flavor, too.*

ENSALADA DE HABA
FRESH FAVA BEAN SALAD

Fava beans aren't native to Mexico—they were brought by the Spaniards after the conquest—but they've been roundly embraced over the course of hundreds of years. They're often used in soups and stews around the country, but my favorite way to eat them is in this simple salad, where young unpeeled fava beans are tossed with olive oil, salt and cilantro. (The amount of cilantro here may seem like a lot, but it's what makes the salad shine.) This makes a hearty side dish with a few tacos, or a filling snack.

1 If using whole fava beans still in their husks, remove the husks and place the beans in a bowl, their waxy inner peels intact.

2 Fill a small saucepan halfway with water. Add the onion half and ½ teaspoon salt and bring to a boil.

3 Add the fava beans and lower the heat to medium. Cook until the beans are tender, 3 to 5 minutes, depending on the bean size. Don't overcook them or else the beans will turn mushy. Drain the beans and let cool to room temperature.

4 Rinse the diced onion briefly in cold water. Drain and add to the beans, along with the chopped cilantro and olive oil. Stir well and season with more salt. Serve immediately.

4 pounds fava beans still in their husks, or 1½ pounds husked very young fava beans with the waxy peel still on
½ small onion plus 2 tablespoons diced
salt
12 stems fresh cilantro, coarsely chopped
2 tablespoons mild olive oil

COOKING TIP: *Older fava beans will taste bitter or leathery if the skin's left on. Young beans have a firm, pleasant bite. Look for favas that have a delicate, almost mint-green color in the pod and avoid yellowish-green or brown-speckled beans, which are too old and won't taste right. You could also try peeling the favas for this salad, but the flavor will be creamier and nuttier, and might need a spritz of lime juice.*

PAMBAZOS
FRIED CHORIZO AND POTATO SANDWICHES

For a good while after I moved to Mexico City, the pambazo *scared me. It was a decadent, fried sandwich, oozing crema and lumps of chorizo and potatoes, not meant for weight-conscious gringas. But after a year of passing these guajillo-painted rolls, I caved and ordered one at a market in the Centro Histórico.*

The young woman behind the counter grabbed a roll and placed it in a bubbling fryer. She scooped out the bread with a slotted spoon and transferred it to a cutting board, where she split the bread into two pieces with her fingers. On one side she added a spatula full of chorizo and potato that she had warmed on the grill. "Con todo?" she asked. I nodded. Over the potato, she poured one spoonful of crema, then a second, then a third. Then she sprinkled on shredded lettuce, and finally, added the other side of the bread.

I bit into the sandwich. The bread crunched slightly. The meaty, salty filling I'd expected to go down like a sloppy joe tasted somehow light. Cool. I ate the whole thing and my pambazo *fear evaporated, along with any leftover crumbs.*

4 Yukon Gold or any other small waxy potato (1½ pounds total), peeled

2 teaspoons lard or canola oil, plus more for frying

½ small white onion, chopped

2 medium cloves garlic, minced

8 ounces Mexican chorizo, casings removed

salt

4 day-old Mexican *telera* rolls, or hoagie or kaiser rolls

½ cup Homemade Crema (page 139)

1 to 2 cups shredded iceberg lettuce

For the sauce:

5 guajillo chiles, seeded, deveined and toasted briefly on a *comal*

¼ cup chopped onion

1 small garlic clove, peeled

½ teaspoon salt, or more to taste

1 Place the potatoes in a medium pot and cover them with 2 inches cold water. Bring to a boil and simmer on high until the potatoes are soft when pierced with a fork, 28 to 30 minutes. Let cool, then dice.

2 Meanwhile, make the sauce: Hydrate the toasted chiles in water until the skins are soft, about 20 minutes. Transfer, with ½ cup of the chile water (see sidebar), into a blender jar with the onion, garlic and salt. Blend until mostly smooth, stopping occasionally to scrape down the sides of the blender jar. The sauce won't be completely silky-smooth. That's okay. Taste again and add more salt if desired.

3 Heat the lard in a large skillet over medium heat. Add the onion and cook until translucent, about 3 minutes. Add the garlic, stirring until sizzling and aromatic, about 30 seconds, and then add the chorizo, breaking it apart into small crumbles. Raise the heat to medium-high and stir often until the sausage is cooked through, 8 to 10 minutes.

4 Stir in the potato and salt to taste. Cook until warmed through, cover and keep warm.

5 Cut each roll in half and remove some of the inner crumb. Brush the outer crust of each roll with a light coating of the chile sauce. Working in batches, warm 2 teaspoons lard or canola oil in a cast-iron skillet over medium heat. When smoking, add one half of the bread, chile-sauce side down. Cook until dark-golden brown and crisp, about 3 minutes. Remove and add the other piece of bread, also chile-sauce side down. Repeat with the remaining rolls, draining between batches on a wire rack set on top of a baking sheet.

6 To serve, spoon about ½ cup of the warm chorizo and potato mixture onto one bread half, then top with a layer of crema and a fistful of lettuce. Cover with the other piece of bread. Repeat with the remaining pieces of bread and serve immediately, while the bread is still crunchy and hot.

WHY CHILE WATER INSTEAD OF REGULAR WATER?

Chile water is the term I use for the flavorful water left over from soaking dried chiles. I use it often to thin out sauces or salsas, as it adds a slight pop of heat. Be careful, though—if you burn your chiles, the water will taste bitter, and if the chiles are very hot, the water may be too spicy to use. It's best to taste a little before you add it to anything.

COOKING TIPS: *Using a cast-iron skillet gives the bread an even, golden-brown toast. I chose Yukon Gold potatoes because they're richer than russets, but the latter will work. Use radish greens and cilantro for a more vibrant substitution for the lettuce. Lastly, be careful when selecting Mexican chorizo—processed varieties can taste over-seasoned. The best ones are made by the butchers themselves. If you're unsure, ask.*

FLAUTAS DE RES
STEAK FLAUTAS

Flautas, or "flutes," common to Northern Mexico and Guadalajara, are long, fried corn tortilla tubes, usually topped with a messy handful of lettuce or cabbage and a squirt of lime juice and salsa. They're very common in Mexico City street stands and markets, with vendors frying them up in huge, bowl-shaped fryers. The filling—bits of simply seasoned shredded steak or chicken—is plain but delicious. You don't need to overthink it, particularly if you have a great salsa on the side. My personal favorite is Chile Pasilla Salsa, and the recipe opposite is inspired by a local flauta market stand. This will serve at least four with a side such as Basic Cooked Beans (page 107) or Mexican-style Red Rice (page 97).

In the United States, we generally call any sort of fried, tube-shaped taco a taquito. In Mexico City, these snacks have different names, depending on their shape. Longer fried tubes—measuring the length of a dinner plate—are called flautas. *Their shorter cousins, made from standard-size corn tortillas, are called* tacos dorados. Taquitos, *meanwhile, mean "small tacos" in Mexico City, and don't refer to a rolled-up snack at all.*

1½ pounds beef chuck roast
¼ medium onion
1 large garlic clove, unpeeled
salt and freshly ground black
    pepper
15 to 20 corn tortillas
1 cup vegetable oil
2 cups Homemade Crema
    (page 139)
1 cup crumbled queso fresco
Chile Pasilla Salsa (recipe
    follows)
2 cups chopped cabbage
4 to 5 limes, cut into wedges

1   Place the meat, onion, and garlic in a large pot and cover with cold water. Heat to boiling and add a heaping teaspoon of salt. Simmer gently for about 2 hours, or until tender when pulled apart with a fork. Transfer the meat to a cutting board to cool. Once cool enough to handle, shred the meat finely. Taste and season with salt and pepper. Strain the broth and save for another use, discarding the onion and garlic.

2   Warm the corn tortillas a few at a time on a *comal* or in a nonstick skillet, until soft and pliable. Remove to a dishcloth to keep warm.

3   Place one tortilla on your work surface. Grab a small handful of meat and arrange in a long rectangle in the center of the tortilla. Roll into a tight tube and secure closed with a toothpick. Repeat with the remaining tortillas and meat.

4   Set a wire rack on a baking sheet next to the stove. Heat the vegetable oil in a large heavy skillet over medium-high heat. (To tell when the oil is ready, tear off a dime-size piece of tortilla and add it to the oil; if the piece bubbles and sizzles, the oil is ready.)

5   Add the *flautas* about four at a time, depending on the size of your pan, and fry about 1 minute per side, turning occasionally with tongs, until golden brown all around. Transfer to the wire rack to drain. Repeat with the remaining *flautas*.

6   Serve warm, topped first with a layer of crema and cheese, then salsa, then cabbage. Pass the lime wedges at the table.

COOKING TIP: *I use standard-size corn tortillas here because they're easiest for home cooks to find. Most Mexicans, however, would say that these are no longer* flautas *but* tacos dorados. *Either way, don't overcook the tortillas or they won't roll. Leftover poached, shredded chicken or brisket would also work swimmingly instead of steak, and you can bake the* flautas *instead of frying them for a toastier, healthier dish.*

CHILE PASILLA SALSA

The charred, bitter notes of this salsa match wonderfully with steak, but you can also use it on anything else you'd like: eggs, quesadillas or other meat tacos. Store in an airtight container for up to one week. (The salsa will mellow over time.)

1   Heat a *comal*, griddle or skillet to medium-low heat. Place the chiles at the edge of the *comal* and turn constantly for 5 to 10 seconds, until colored and softened. Place the chiles in a bowl of warm water and let sit until the skins soften, about 20 minutes; reserve the soaking water. Meanwhile, place the garlic near the edge of the *comal* and turn occasionally until soft and blackened in spots, 5 to 7 minutes, then set aside to cool. Increase the heat to medium-high and add the tomatoes, turning often with tongs, until soft and blackened in spots.

2   Peel the garlic cloves and place in a blender jar with the chiles and ¼ cup of the reserved chile water. Pulse until a thick paste forms, then scrape the sides of the blender jar and pulse a bit more. Add the tomatoes and salt. Pulse a few more times until the tomatoes break down but the salsa is still rather chunky. Taste for seasoning and add salt if needed.

3   Pour the salsa into a serving bowl and set on the table for guests to serve themselves extra if desired.

6 pasilla chiles, stemmed and
  seeded
2 large cloves garlic, unpeeled
4 ripe plum tomatoes
1½ teaspoons salt

HUARACHES DE FLOR DE CALABAZA
SQUASH FLOWER HUARACHES

Huaraches—named for their long, oval shape, like the sole of a leather sandal—were invented near Mexico City's Jamaica Market, according to local legend. Shops specializing in huaraches *still operate near the market today. The masa is predominantly shaped by women, who grab handfuls of the sticky corn dough, toss it on the flat-top grill, and quickly spread it into shape with their fingers. The modern* huarache *is monstrous: a masa boat the length of a dinner plate, stuffed with a thin layer of black beans and topped with stewed meat or vegetables, crema, avocado and a thick layer of melted cheese. You can order almost any combination of toppings you want, but my favorites usually contain vegetables—mushrooms, squash flowers, poblano peppers. These are fun to serve at dinner parties, once you get comfortable shaping the masa. To do so, you'll need a rolling pin and a plain plastic grocery bag cut into two large pieces.*

1 batch Quick Refried Beans
  (page 45)

1 batch Chile Morita Salsa (recipe
  follows), for serving

4 poblano peppers

2 pounds fresh tortilla masa

¼ cup room-temperature water,
  plus more as needed

1 tablespoon canola oil

½ cup chopped onion

2 medium cloves garlic, minced

1 bunch fresh squash blossoms,
  stems removed and flowers
  torn in half (about 4 cups)

3 cups sliced crimini mushrooms,
  or 1 (8-ounce) package

1 bunch epazote, leaves only

½ teaspoon salt, or more to taste

2 cups shredded quesillo or any
  other mild, melty cheese

2 cups Homemade Crema
  (page 139)

1   Prepare the refried beans and salsa and set aside.

2   Roast, peel and seed the poblano peppers (see instructions on page 37). Chop into 1½-inch by ¼-inch strips and set aside.

3   Place the masa in a large deep bowl and add the water a few tablespoons at a time, kneading extensively after each addition until the dough is extremely sticky and stretchy. You may need between ¼ and ½ cup water, depending on the humidity, altitude and other factors. Cover the dough with a damp dishcloth while you prepare the filling.

4   Heat the oil in a large skillet over medium heat. Add the onion and cook until translucent, 3 minutes, then add the garlic and cook until aromatic, about 30 seconds. Add the squash flowers and mushrooms and cook, stirring occasionally, until the squash flowers are tender and the mushrooms are cooked through, 3 to 5 minutes. Stir in the epazote leaves, poblano peppers and salt. Remove from the heat and set aside.

5   Heat a *comal* or griddle over medium heat. Create a workspace with the refried beans, dough, a rolling pin and plastic grocery bags. Dampen your hands with water. Grab a chunk of masa and roll into a ball slightly smaller than a billiard ball. Create a small crater in the ball with your thumbs and fill with a spoonful of refried beans. Press closed by folding the dough around the beans, and roll again into a ball, then flatten into a thick rectangular shape with your palms.

6   Place one sheet of plastic on the cutting board, and put the oval patty in the middle. Cover with a second sheet of plastic. Use a rolling pin to roll out the *huarache* into a long sole-of-your-shoe shape, about 8 inches long and ¼ inch thick.

7   Dampen your hands again. Carefully peel back the top layer of plastic, and flip the *huarache* into your upturned hand, positioning it so that half hangs off. Carefully peel back the top layer of plastic—the *huarache* may stretch a bit while it's hanging there. Moving your hand in a swift left-to-right motion, place the *huarache* on the hot *comal*.

8 Cook until the edges darken slightly, 1 to 2 minutes, then flip and cook a few minutes more. Lower the heat and cook, turning occasionally, until the masa inside is no longer raw and the outside is slightly crisp and speckled with dark-golden spots, 12 to 15 minutes or slightly longer depending on your stove. (If the center of the *comal* is very hot, you may need to move the *huarache* away from direct heat.) Test the first one by cutting it in half. If it's raw in the center, return it to the stove and make a note for next time.

9 Stack the *huaraches* in a clean dishcloth and wrap tightly to keep them warm. Repeat filling, shaping and cooking the remaining *huaraches*.

10 To serve, reheat the vegetable filling and lightly warm the *huaraches* on a *comal* if needed. Spread the morita salsa in a thin layer on top of the *huarache*, followed by a thick layer of vegetable filling. Top with shredded cheese. If *huaraches* are no longer hot and the cheese doesn't melt right away, place them in a broiler for a minute or two. Serve immediately, passing more salsa and the crema at the table.

COOKING TIPS: *Quesillo, an acidic cow's-milk cheese traditional to Oaxaca, is the typical* huarache *topping, but it's hard to find good-quality quesillo in the U.S. Feel free to use any other mild, melty cheese as a substitute. If you can't find squash flowers—available in mid- to late-summer in many farmer's markets—use 2 cups fresh corn kernels.*

A moist, almost wet masa is essential here, or else the huaraches *will dry out and turn into crackers as they cook. The dough should be much moister than tortillas and it may even stretch a little once it reaches the desired consistency. Damp hands are important as is a steady even heat. Masa harina is not an adequate substitute here. The flour doesn't soak up the necessary liquid, and the* huaraches *taste crumbly.*

CHILE MORITA SALSA

This smoky, intense salsa, inspired by a version I tried near the Jamaica Market, jazzes up the huaraches *and pretty much anything else it touches. (It's also fairly salty, but it needs that to stand up to the* huarache *filling.) The salsa will keep in the refrigerator in an airtight container for up to a week.*

1 small plum tomato
1 medium garlic clove, unpeeled
6 morita chiles
salt

1 Heat a *comal* or nonstick skillet to medium heat. Add the tomato in the center and the garlic clove near the edge. Cook until they're soft and blackened in spots, 5 to 7 minutes.

2 Meanwhile, briefly toast the chiles for about 30 seconds per side, just enough for them to soften and release their aromas. Remove the chiles to a bowl filled with hot water. Let them sit for about 20 minutes or until the skins soften.

3 Remove the stems and add the chiles to a blender jar with the garlic, tomato and ¼ cup water. Pulse into a thick sauce. Pour into a bowl and season with salt. Serve at room temperature.

ENSALADA DE NOPAL
CACTUS SALAD

Most markets sell a small number of prepared foods to go, like cactus salad, which is prepared fresh daily and sold by the kilo from big, colorful ceramic platters or clay pots. The salad—a mix of cooked cactus, cilantro, onion, and Mexican oregano—is most often eaten as a side dish. You can find variations of it in several other Mexican states, including Tlaxcala and Puebla. The dish is so common that there's really no official recipe, but it should taste fresh and bright and balanced, with a hint of spice from the oregano. Some people add fresh chile, others more cheese, and I've even heard of adding pumpkin seeds, although I personally don't think it needs them. Here, I've added tomatoes.

12 cactus paddles, rinsed, spines removed (see sidebar)

¼ large onion, sliced into thin slivers

salt and freshly ground black pepper

½ cup coarsely chopped fresh cilantro

2 plum tomatoes, seeded and diced, or 24 grape tomatoes, sliced in half

2 tablespoons olive oil

½ heaping teaspoon Mexican oregano

½ cup crumbled queso fresco, or other mild farmer's cheese

COOKING TIP: *Cactus naturally oozes a light slime, similar to okra, but most of it should seep out during cooking.*

1 Bring a pot of water to boil. While you're waiting, cut the cactus paddles into ¼-inch by 1½-inch strips.

2 Add the cactus, onion slivers, and a pinch of salt to the water and cook them for 6 to 8 minutes, stirring occasionally, until the cactus is tender and turns a dull green color. Strain, discarding the cooking water but keeping the onion slivers. Let the cactus cool to room temperature.

3 Place the cactus and onion in a serving bowl. Add the cilantro, tomatoes, oil, ¼ teaspoon pepper, the oregano, and the queso fresco and toss to combine. Taste and add ½ teaspoon salt, then mix again, and taste for more salt if necessary.

4 Serve immediately, or chill for up to 2 hours.

HOW TO CLEAN A CACTUS PADDLE

Unless you don't mind the idea of thorns in your skin, wear rubber gloves or wrap your non-dominant hand—the one that holds the cactus paddle—in a dish towel.

1. *With your hands protected, place a cactus paddle on a cutting board, the narrower end toward you.*
2. *Steadying the paddle on the narrow end, carefully cut off the very outer edge of the cactus paddle. (These spines generally are too hard to remove one by one.)*
3. *Pick up the paddle and hold it at a 45-degree angle. Angle a sharp knife and scrape off the spines, cutting so they fall away from you. Flip to scrape the other side, until all spines have been removed.*
4. *Cut off the rough end near the paddle base. Rinse the paddle in cold water. See the photos on page 146.*

RAJAS CON CREMA
ROASTED POBLANO PEPPERS WITH MEXICAN CREAM

At the same market stands that sell ready-made cactus and fava bean salads, you can often find rajas con crema, a mixture of roasted, peeled poblano peppers, Mexican cream and cheese. As an American, this mix reminds me a lot of what I love about casseroles: it's buttery and comforting, with a touch of heat from the chiles. My version is not as rich as what's sometimes sold in Mexico City, but it communicates the same decadent idea. In Mexico, these are generally eaten in tacos, or with rice and beans or a soup to make it a meal. You could also stir these into pasta, spoon them onto eggs, or eat them on hunks of toasted French bread.

8 chiles poblanos, charred and seeded (see page 37)
1 to 2 tablespoons canola oil
½ cup chopped onion
2 medium cloves garlic, minced
½ cup chicken or vegetable stock
salt
¼ cup plus 2 tablespoons Homemade Crema (page 139)
scant ¼ cup grated Monterrey Jack, or other mild, melty cheese
8 to 12 corn tortillas
salsa of choice

1 Cut the chiles into ¼-inch by 1½-inch strips. (You can prepare the chiles up to 1 day ahead of time.)

2 In a medium skillet, heat the oil over medium heat until shimmering. Add the onion and cook until soft and translucent, 3 to 5 minutes. Add the garlic and cook until aromatic, 1 minute.

3 Stir in the poblano peppers, stock and a few pinches of salt. Cook until the peppers are warmed and a bit more tender, 2 to 3 minutes. (Don't overcook them or they'll get limp and slimy.)

4 Mix in the crema and cheese, stirring until the cheese melts. Remove the pan from heat and season the *rajas* with salt, if desired.

5 Allowing at least two to three per person, warm the tortillas on a *comal* or in the microwave, wrapped in paper towels, until soft and pliable. Place the tortillas in a dishcloth or basket to keep warm.

6 Heat up the *rajas con crema* if needed, and scrape into a serving bowl. Pass the bowl and the warm tortillas, along with your desired salsa.

QUELITES SUDADOS
"SWEATED" MEXICAN GREENS

Quelite is a catch-all word for any native Mexican green with young, tender leaves. Lambs quarters, known in Mexico City as quelite cenizo, are popular in markets, and so are quintoniles, or amaranth greens. They're almost always eaten simply—steamed with a little onion, garlic and chile, and spooned into freshly made tortillas. One of my favorite things about quelites (besides their nutrient-rich profile) is that they have a thicker texture than, say, spinach. Even after cooking, they retain a certain bite. They also tend to be grassier, slightly sweeter and more aromatic than any other green I've tasted. These work great as a side dish to a meat-heavy meal. They also make a wonderful quesadilla filling; just be sure to warm the cooked greens briefly on a comal or skillet to evaporate some of the water, so the tortillas don't turn mushy and fall apart.

1 Heat the oil in large skillet over medium heat.

2 Add the onion, garlic and chile, stirring constantly until the onions are translucent, about 3 minutes.

3 Add the *quelites*—in batches, if necessary—and season with salt and pepper to taste. Stir with tongs to coat in the onion mix. Lower the heat to medium-low and cover tightly, letting the leaves release their natural juices until they're limp but still somewhat al dente, 3 to 5 minutes. (Spinach may take less time, about 2 minutes.) Season with more salt and pepper if needed and remove from the heat.

4 Allowing at least two to three per person, warm the tortillas on a *comal* or in the microwave, wrapped in paper towels, until soft and pliable. Place in a dishcloth or basket to keep warm.

5 Heat up the *quelites* if needed and transfer to a serving bowl. Pass the bowl of steamed *quelites* with the warm tortillas, along with desired salsa and lime wedges.

1 tablespoon olive oil
¼ small onion, cut into slivers
2 large cloves garlic, minced
½ serrano chile, minced, with seeds (use less if you don't want any heat)
2 pounds *quelites* (or spinach or chard; see Tip), rinsed well and drained
salt and freshly ground black pepper
8 to 12 corn tortillas
salsa of choice
lime wedges

COOKING TIP: *For the quelites to steam adequately, you'll need a large skillet with a lid. Some farmers' markets carry lambs quarters and amaranth greens in the spring and summer. Chinese markets may also carry amaranth greens. If you can't find quelites, substitute spinach or chard. (And don't discard the chard stems—they're great chopped and sautéed with the onion.)*

TACOS CAMPECHANOS
STEAK AND CHORIZO TACOS

The word campechano *in Mexican cooking often refers to a mixing of something—light and dark beer, for instance (*una cerveza campechana*); two types of seafood in a cocktail (*un cóctel campechano*); and, perhaps most popularly, in tacos that feature both steak and chorizo. You can find tacos campechanos at taquerías all over the city, and all over the country. This recipe was inspired by a taco I had at a tianguis south of the city center, where the steak—a thin, salty, aged cut called* cecina*—was cooked on an open flame and topped with crumbly chorizo, a dollop of crema and a handful of Pico de Gallo Salsa. The flavors and textures left an impression, and luckily they're fairly easy to re-create at home.*

13 ounces chorizo
1 pound thinly sliced *cecina* steak (see Tip)
12 corn tortillas
3 limes, cut into wedges
Pico de Gallo Salsa (see opposite)
½ cup Homemade Crema (page 139)

1   Heat a large cast-iron skillet over medium heat. Use a knife to delicately slice into each chorizo's outer casing. Peel off the casing and discard. Add the chorizo to the skillet and crumble into small pieces. Cook uncovered, stirring occasionally, until crisp-edged, firm and darker in color, 8 to 10 minutes. Transfer to a plate lined with paper towels.

2   Wipe out the same pan with paper towels. Heat to medium and, when hot, add one piece of *cecina* and cook for 3 minutes without disturbing, or until dark-golden brown spots appear on the underside. Flip and repeat. Transfer the meat to a cutting board and let rest for 3 minutes. Chop the *cecina* into small pieces and set aside.

3   Heat the tortillas on a *comal* until soft and pliable, and keep warm in a dishcloth or covered basket.

4   To serve, place a small handful of chopped *cecina* on the warm tortilla and sprinkle the chorizo on top. Spritz with lime juice, and add a heaping spoonful of pico de gallo. Finish with a dollop of crema. Serve immediately.

COOKING TIP: *Outside of Mexico City,* cecina *is widely consumed in Morelos, Puebla and Oaxaca, among other states. Most Mexican grocery stores in the U.S. carry* cecina *in the butcher department. Buy the thinnest variety you can find and cook it on a grill if possible, or, as a second choice, a blazing hot cast-iron skillet. If you can't find* cecina*, a thin skirt steak would work.*

SALSA DE PICO DE GALLO
FRESH TOMATO SALSA

In Southern California, pico de gallo *refers to the spicy chile powder sprinkled on cut fruit or jicama. In Mexico City, as in other areas of Mexico, the name means a fresh, chunky salsa of ripe tomatoes, white onion and any sort of fresh green chile—jalapeño, serrano or fresh árbol chile, depending on how hot you want it.*

This is a rustic dish, so there's no right way to make it. You want a juicy, tangy, citrusy mix, with plenty of bite from the fresh cilantro. This makes quite a bit—but it will disappear faster than you think. I like this on Steak and Chorizo Tacos (see opposite) or spooned onto thick pieces of Homemade Chicharrón (page 136).

1   Place the tomatoes, onion, cilantro and chiles in a bowl. (The pieces shouldn't look too perfect—this is a rustic dish.)

2   Pour in the lime juice and mix well. Season with salt, taste, and add more cilantro or lime juice if needed. Serve immediately.

COOKING TIP: *This salsa will keep for up to two days in an airtight container in the refrigerator, although the flavor will mellow and it may release more liquid, depending on how juicy your tomatoes are. Use a slotted spoon to serve, if necessary.*

2 pounds plum tomatoes, or any other ripe, fresh tomato, diced
½ medium onion, roughly chopped
8 to 12 stems fresh cilantro, roughly chopped
3 large jalapeños or 4 serranos, stemmed and cut into half-moons, with seeds
¼ cup fresh lime juice, or more to taste
salt

POLLO ROSTIZADO EN ADOBO
ROASTED CHICKEN IN ADOBO

Roasted chicken, juicy and golden and rotating on a spit, is a neighborhood specialty in Mexico City. This recipe, for chicken slathered in an aromatic dried-chile adobo, comes from Alonso Ruvalcaba, a food writer who recently opened his own roasted chicken shop in Condesa. The dish is a little fancier than what's sold in chicken joints and market stalls, but he's captured the essence of what makes Mexican chicken so good: a crisp, flavorful, slightly spicy skin and moist flesh. Serve with a stack of warm tortillas, some salsa, and (if you want to be truly authentic) homemade potato chips, so guests can make tacos.

For the chicken and sauce:

1 whole chicken, giblets removed
  (about 4 pounds)
½ teaspoon salt per pound of
  chicken
2 plum tomatoes
½ medium onion
2 cloves garlic, unpeeled
¼ cup raw peanuts
1 (3-inch) cinnamon stick
2 morita chiles
2 guajillo chiles
2 dried árbol chiles
2 dried chipotle chiles
¼ cup white vinegar
1 tablespoon vanilla extract
1 lemon
1 small bunch thyme

For the vegetables:

12 cloves garlic, peeled
12 small red or white potatoes,
  cut in half
6 small beets, cut into quarters,
  or eighths if they're large
2 red onions, peeled and cut
  into eighths
olive oil
salt and freshly ground black
  pepper

1   A day ahead, season the chicken generously with the salt and refrigerate in a covered container for about 4 hours.

2   Meanwhile, warm a *comal* or nonstick skillet to medium-high heat. Add the tomatoes, onion, and garlic and cook until soft and blackened in spots, 4 to 8 minutes.

3   Place 3 cups water in a medium saucepan and bring to a boil.

4   Heat a small skillet to low heat. Toast the peanuts and cinnamon, stirring constantly, until the peanuts turn a golden brown color, 2 to 3 minutes. (If black spots appear, lower the flame.) Transfer to a bowl. Raise the heat to medium and quickly toast the chiles in batches, 5 to 10 seconds per side or until aromatic, careful not to burn them.

5   Snip off the chiles' stems, and shake out the seeds. Add the chiles to the boiling water and cook until the skins soften, about 20 minutes. Transfer to a blender jar, and discard the water. Add the charred tomatoes, onion, garlic, peanuts, cinnamon, vinegar, and vanilla extract. Blend on high into a very smooth, thick paste. Season with salt.

6   Remove the chicken from the refrigerator and drain off any excess liquid. Slather with the adobo sauce, spreading it over and underneath the skin. Place the chicken in a resealable plastic bag and pour any remaining adobo on top. Refrigerate for 24 hours.

7   The next day, bring the chicken to room temperature, uncovered, about 45 minutes. Preheat the oven to 450°F.

8   Place the chicken breast-side up on a V-shaped rack set over a roasting pan. Cut the lemon in half and place it and the thyme in the chicken's cavity. Set the chicken in the middle of your oven and cook for 20 minutes.

9   Toss the vegetables with oil and season with salt and pepper and add to the roasting pan. Lower the temperature to 425°F and cook until the chicken is crispy and the juices run clear, or the internal temperature measures 165°F, about 1 more hour, turning the vegetables occasionally so they don't burn.

10   Let the chicken sit for 15 minutes before serving. Remove the lemon and thyme from the cavity, and slice. Serve with the vegetables.

PENEQUES
BATTERED STUFFED TORTILLAS

Peneques are puffy corn tortilla pockets, sold by the bagful by women at the markets or tianguis. *They seem so unusual—you don't see them on menus anywhere, or at least I haven't—that I actually pondered for a while whether to even include them in this book. But then, on different visits to Mexico City, they seemed to be following me, popping up at market stands I'd never seen before.*

Of course the vendors offered me a recipe: slice them open, stuff them with beans and cheese, and then dunk them in a light egg batter known in Spanish as the capeado. *This is the same batter used for chiles rellenos, and vegetable or meat fritters known as* tortitas. *Interestingly, the tortilla acts as a chile in this case, nestling beans and cheese in its eggy coat.*

My version includes vegetables, which add a bit of snap amid the oozy cheese. The result, drenched in spicy tomato sauce, makes for an extremely dignified meal, made more ingenious considering peneques *can be made from any leftover scraps in the fridge. I like serving these with Basic Cooked Beans (page 107).*

1 batch Ranchera Sauce
   (page 105)
2 teaspoons plus ½ cup
   canola oil
3 tablespoons chopped onion
1 small garlic clove, minced
6 ounces fresh green beans, cut
   into 1½-inch pieces
salt
2 small Mexican squash, sliced
   into ¼-inch-thick half-moons
6 corn tortillas
1 cup shredded Monterey Jack
   cheese
1 teaspoon flour, plus more for
   dredging
5 large eggs, separated

1   Make the ranchera sauce and set aside. The sauce can be made up to 1 day in advance and stored in the refrigerator.

2   Heat 2 teaspoons canola oil over medium heat in a medium skillet. When hot, add the onion and garlic and cook until translucent and aromatic, stirring often, 2 minutes.

3   Add the green beans and a few pinches of salt. Stir well to coat in the onion-garlic mixture, then add a few tablespoons water. Reduce the heat to low, cover and cook until the green beans are just tender, 3 minutes.

4   Add the squash and another pinch of salt, and stir well. Raise the heat back to medium and cook uncovered, stirring often, until tender, 4 minutes. Taste and add more salt if necessary. (You want the filling slightly saltier than you might think, in order for it to stand out inside the tortilla pocket.) Remove from the heat, cover and set aside.

5   Warm the tortillas on a *comal*, crisping them slightly. Place in a dishcloth to keep warm.

6   Create a workspace with the cheese, filling, a small plate with flour for dredging, and the warm tortillas. Place a wire rack on a rimmed baking sheet in a warm oven.

7   Grab a tortilla and fill it with a few pinches of vegetables and one pinch of shredded cheese. Fold the tortilla into a half-moon shape (the filling should not spill out; if it does, you have too much). Dredge both sides lightly in the flour and place on a plate. Repeat with the remaining tortillas.

8   In a medium bowl, whisk the egg whites by hand or with an electric mixer until stiff peaks form. Using a rubber spatula, fold in the egg yolks one by one, and then gently stir in the flour and ½ teaspoon salt.

9 Warm ½ cup canola oil in a large frying pan over medium-high to high heat. To test when it's ready for frying, add a small dab of the egg batter to the pan. If it bubbles and turns golden brown at the edges within 5 to 10 seconds, it's ready. If the batter immediately turns dark brown, the oil is too hot.

10 Once the oil is almost ready, begin warming up your ranchera sauce in a pot over low heat and leave covered while you fry the *peneques*.

11 Give the egg batter one more stir. Then, using both thumbs to pinch the tortilla closed, scoop a *peneque* deeply through the egg batter and place in the hot oil. It should sizzle and puff up into a cloud. Place a dollop of egg batter on the bare space where your thumbs were. Using a spoon, bathe the *peneque* in the hot oil—this will make it easier to flip later. Cook for 20 to 30 seconds, then flip, taking care not to slosh around the hot oil. (If it's easier for you to flip using two spatulas, do it.) Cook for another 30 more seconds, bathing any uncooked sides of the *peneque* in oil, until golden brown. Transfer to the wire rack in the oven to drain. (The egg may deflate a little upon serving, but that's okay.) Repeat with the remaining *peneques*. Alternatively, serve the hot *peneque* immediately.

12 To serve, place one *peneque* on a plate and ladle enough ranchera sauce on top to completely cover it.

COOKING TIPS: *Puffy tortilla pockets are next to impossible to find outside Mexico, so I use regular corn tortillas here. Mastering the correct way to dunk an item in the capeado takes practice if you've never done it before. The egg whites should be fluffy and frothy, and the yolks completely integrated. Make space for your batter bowl near the stove, so you don't drip batter across the kitchen floor.*

HUEVOS A LA MEXICANA
MEXICAN-STYLE EGGS

1 tablespoon canola oil
½ cup chopped onion
1 garlic clove, minced
1 serrano chile, seeded and minced (or keep
    seeds in for more heat)
salt
2 ripe plum tomatoes, chopped
8 large eggs, beaten lightly with
    ¼ teaspoon salt
corn tortillas
salsa of choice, optional

Many Mexican market stands that serve breakfast don't have menus, so when you arrive, after the obligatory "Buenos días" greeting, it's customary to plop yourself down on a stool and ask, "Qué hay?" (What is there?). The reply is usually a recitation of delicious-sounding items: "Mire, tenemos riquísimas enchiladas verdes. Tenemos sopes preparados, y huevos al gusto. Lo que usted desea." Translation: "Look, we have delicious green enchiladas. We have sopes with all the toppings, and eggs any way you like. Whatever you wish."

Huevos a la Mexicana—usually lumped under the heading al gusto, or the customer's preference—was the first breakfast dish I learned to order at a market on my own, and it quickly became a favorite for its simple mix of egg, tomato, chile, and onion. (Sometimes my stomach can't handle enchilada sauce at ten in the morning.)

1   Heat the oil in a medium skillet over medium heat.

2   When hot, add the onion, garlic, and chile and a pinch of salt. Cook until translucent, about 3 minutes.

3   Add the chopped tomato and ¼ teaspoon salt. Cook until the tomatoes are tender but not yet breaking down into a paste, about 3 minutes.

4   Lower the heat and stir in the eggs. Stir constantly, gently folding the eggs over themselves, until they scramble. If the eggs turn brown, lower the flame or remove the pan from the heat. Cook until the eggs are fluffy and no longer wet.

5   Serve with warm corn tortillas and salsa, if desired.

TAMALES DE ELOTE
SWEET CORN TAMALES

Sweet corn tamales are a mainstay at the weekly tianguis, *sold at the same stands that offer fresh corn tortillas, tlacoyos, and sopes. They're smaller than the big, dense tamales sold on the street, so they're perfect as a snack or light breakfast. The corn flavor should shine, so it's best to use both fresh sweet corn and fresh masa for tamales, if you can find them. (If you're buying from a tortillería, make sure the masa does not contain lard.) Otherwise, frozen corn and masa harina are acceptable substitutes. Serve these with a little crema on the side, or Chile Pasilla Salsa (page 73) if you like sweet and savory things. For steamer pot instructions, see page 37.*

1   To make the masa, in a small saucepan, gently warm the milk—either 5 cups or ½ cup—until it's just a notch above lukewarm. Turn off the heat.

2   If using masa harina, in a large deep bowl, whisk together the masa harina, baking powder and salt. Slowly add the 5 cups warmed milk, incorporating the liquid thoroughly. You should end up with a moist, cohesive dough. Set aside for 10 minutes. Alternatively, if using fresh masa, pour the ½ cup warmed milk over the dough and knead lightly until moist and soft. Cover with a damp dishcloth.

3   Using a stand mixer, cream the butter and sugar (amounts dependent on the type of masa you're using) for about 5 minutes until fluffy and lighter in color. With the mixer running on high, add the masa mixture, small bits at a time. Mix well after each addition, scraping the sides of the bowl to make sure the masa incorporates thoroughly. Keep mixing until a sticky, cohesive dough forms, similar to a thick muffin batter. Don't worry about the dough seeming too wet or sticky—it will steam up later in the pot.

4   If using fresh masa, add the baking powder and salt now, mixing well. Taste and see if the dough needs more salt, keeping in mind that steaming will mute the saltiness factor just a bit.

5   The masa should be kept at room temperature until ready to use. If it's very hot in the kitchen, chill it in the refrigerator. Masa made with masa harina can be stored for up to 24 hours in the fridge. Fresh masa must be used the same day or it will turn sour.

6   Soak the corn husks in a big pot of hot water for at least 30 minutes.

7   Add the corn to a food processor and pulse a few times until thick and chunky. Transfer to a bowl and stir in the sugar and salt. Little by little, stir the corn mixture into the masa. Taste for salt and add more if necessary.

8   Assemble and steam the tamales as per the instructions in steps 5 through 12 on pages 36–37.

For masa made with masa harina:

5 cups whole milk, at room temperature

6 cups masa harina for tamales

3 teaspoons baking powder

1¼ teaspoons salt

1½ cups (3 sticks) unsalted butter, at room temperature

½ cup raw or dark brown sugar

For fresh masa:

½ cup whole milk, at room temperature

4 pounds fresh masa for tamales

1¾ cups (3½ sticks) unsalted butter, at room temperature

¾ cup raw or dark brown sugar

3 teaspoons baking powder

1¼ teaspoons salt

at least 36 corn husks

4 cups fresh or frozen sweet corn, thawed

1 cup raw or dark brown sugar

1¼ teaspoons salt

Homemade Crema (page 139) or salsa of choice, for serving

GELATINA DE NARANJA CON MEZCAL
CREAMY ORANGE GELATIN WITH MEZCAL

Plump single-size gelatins—both milk- and water-based—are often sold on the streets, from small glass cases that vendors carry or tote on their backs, or in markets. They come in tropical fruit flavors (mamey, guava, coconut) or they're mixed with nuts or even sherry. Often they're eaten on the go, wrapped in a square of wax paper. The base of this recipe comes from my friend Graciela Montaño, a Mexico City native who teaches cooking classes and makes gelatins in her spare time. I particularly like serving this gelatin after a spicy entrée. An orange sauce or syrup would work nicely drizzled on top, although it's not necessary.

1   The day before you'd like to eat the gelatins, pour ½ cup cold water into a bowl and sprinkle the gelatin powder on top. Let sit while you continue on to the next steps.

2   Pour the cream and milk into a small saucepan and heat to medium-low. Stir in the sugar until dissolved, and then add the orange zest.

3   When the mixture just starts to boil, add the mezcal or tequila and cook for 3 minutes to let the flavors combine.

4   Remove the pot from the heat and whisk in the gelatin until it's no longer lumpy.

5   Place the gelatin molds or tray on top of a baking sheet, and whisk the gelatin mixture once more to make sure the zest is evenly distributed. Using a ladle, pour the hot gelatin gently into each mold. Let cool 20 minutes, then refrigerate overnight.

6   When ready to serve, remove the molds from the refrigerator and bring them slightly to room temperature, about 15 minutes. Use a butter knife to delicately release the sides of each gelatin. Place a baking tray on top of your molds, and flip. Let gelatins release from the molds on their own, or if using silicone, you can gently push them out.

7   Scoop the gelatins onto small serving dishes and serve cold. Extra gelatins will keep wrapped in plastic wrap or an airtight container for up to a week.

1 envelope powdered gelatin, such as Knox (about 1 scant tablespoon)
1½ cups heavy cream
½ cup whole milk
¼ cup plus 1 tablespoon sugar
1 teaspoon orange zest
2 teaspoons mezcal or tequila, or more to taste

COOKING TIP: *You can use either individual metal molds for this dish or a silicone tray outfitted with six separate cups. I like silicone because it's naturally non-stick. If you use metal molds, rinse them in cold water beforehand and store them in the refrigerator while you cook—this step will make the gelatin easier to dislodge later.*

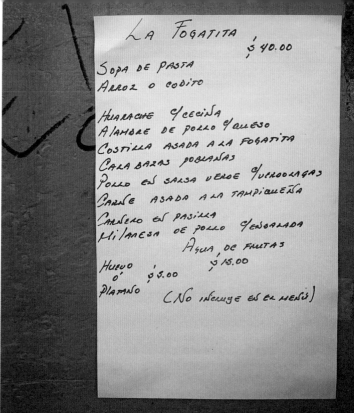

La Fogatita $40.00

Sopa de Pasta
Arroz o Codito

Huarache c/cecina
Alambre de pollo y queso
Costilla asada a la Fogatita
Calabazas Poblanas
Pollo en salsa verde c/chochoyagas
Carne asada a la tampiqueña
Carnero en pasilla
Milanesa de pollo c/ensalada
              Agua de Frutas
Huevo $15.00
  o $5.00
Platano   (No incluye en el menú)

PARRILLA
Alambre c/queso
Alambre mixto c/queso
Alambre de pollo c/queso
Alambre de chuleta c/queso
Parrillada mixta c/queso
TACOS ORDEN
Pollo c/queso
Bistec c/queso
Costilla c/queso
Chuleta c/queso

CHAPTER 3

IN
THE
FONDAS

In Mexico City on any given day, you'll find a written record of what many people eat for lunch, taped onto stoplights and telephone poles. The papers neatly list three courses from nearby *fondas*, or small homestyle restaurants: a vegetable or chicken soup to start; a "dry" soup (*sopa seca*), such as rice or noodles to follow; then a heavy main course—green enchiladas, liver and onions, a spicy beef *mole de olla*, or *chiles rellenos*, for instance. This meal, sold at an economical price with a warm basket of tortillas, is called *comida corrida*, and it's designed to keep you full until dinnertime. The only required condiments are table salsas (*salsas de mesa)*, which are plunked on the table shortly after you sit down and designed to be spooned on top of your meal.

For a long time I didn't like *comida corrida*, simply because I thought it was too much food. Who eats three courses for lunch? But eventually I warmed to the tradition, and the fleeting daily menu that tomorrow would be ripped down, replaced and forgotten. (*Fondas* rotate their menus, but they do not repeat them two days in a row.) Seeing these *comida corrida* menus as living historical documents, I started snapping pictures of them. As my photo collection grew, I got over my fear and wandered inside, where I found several more things to love.

A MEAL TO LINGER OVER

Comida corrida—and, generally, lunch in Mexico—is lingered over. No one rushes anybody. A pitcher of *aguas frescas* is brought to the table, so you can refill your glass yourself. One hour can stretch into two, or even three. The tortilla basket is continually filled, the salsas sit on the table throughout the afternoon and still taste freshly made.

Many of these dishes have been eaten in Mexico for at least 100 years, a fact I learned after researching in the local gastronomy library. They may not taste as they once did, but to this American, the food is still soul-nourishing. Pork ribs dunked in a dish of *verdolagas en salsa verde* slip off the bone. *Mole verde* demands multiple tortillas to soak up the cuminy, herbal sauce. *Bistec en salsa pasilla* soothes you with its thick, brick-colored bitterness. Dessert at the *fondas*, generally flan or rice pudding, sometimes feels like an afterthought, but most people don't go there for dessert anyway. It's the tradition of the three-course meal, the low price, and the familiarity that draws customers, starting with the little paper menu fluttering on a telephone pole.

AGUA DE JAMAICA
HIBISCUS FLOWER TEA

Purplish-red dried hibiscus flowers, called flores de jamaica *in Spanish, can be bought cheaply and abundantly year-round in Mexico. They're steeped in a tea and served cold or at room temperature at nearly every* fonda *in Mexico City. The taste is sweet and floral and slightly acidic.*

1½ cups dried hibiscus flowers
⅔ cup sugar, or other sweetener,
    such as agave syrup, to taste
fresh lime juice, optional

1   Pick out any twigs from your flowers and rinse briefly in cold water to remove any dust or grit.

2   Bring 2 quarts water to a boil. Add the flowers and cook for 5 minutes, stirring occasionally.

3   Stir in the sugar and cook for a few minutes until dissolved. Turn off the heat. Let cool to room temperature, then strain the tea into a pitcher and add lime juice, if using. Refrigerate or serve over ice.

COOKING TIP: *Outside of Mexico, the quality of hibiscus can vary—some may not taste like anything at all, and others may be slightly gritty. You can find dried hibiscus flowers at Mexican supermarkets, and occasionally at health food or organic markets.*

SALSA DE JALAPEÑO
CREAMY JALAPEÑO SALSA

This green, creamy table salsa is so good, I have to restrain myself from eating it like pudding. The recipe comes from a fonda in the Roma neighborhood called Con Sabor a Tixtla, run by a family from Tixtla, Guerrero. The only ingredients are olive oil, onions and jalapeños, but the sauce tastes much more complex. There are two small tricks: you should blend it for several minutes and you can't, under any circumstances, have a spot of water in your blender jar—if you do, the folks at Con Sabor a Tixtla insist the sauce won't come together. I've never tested the theory. The smell of jalapeños, onions, and garlic browning in olive oil is enough to send me wiping down my blender jar with dish towels.

generous ½ cup olive oil
4 jalapeños, stems removed
2 medium or large garlic cloves,
    peeled
2 (½-inch-thick) slices of onion
¼ teaspoon salt, or more to taste

1   Heat the oil in a large saucepan over medium or medium-low heat. When hot, add the jalapeños, garlic and onion—they should sizzle in the pan; if not, turn up the heat. Turn everything frequently with tongs until the jalapeño skins loosen, whiten slightly and char a bit, and the garlic and olive oil turn a splotchy caramel color, 5 to 7 minutes. (Don't wear your best clothes, as this can splatter.)

2   Let cool for 20 minutes, then pour into a blender jar and add the salt. Blend on high until the salsa looks creamy and no longer mottled, about 4 minutes. Serve immediately.

SOPA SECA DE ARROZ
MEXICAN-STYLE RED RICE

Mexican rice, deepened to a red color by a fresh tomato purée, is the classic second course at fondas, served after soup and before the main meal. In Mexico City, it's often called sopa seca, *or dry soup. Like most Mexican rice preparations, the rice is fried first in oil, and it's customary to add a few vegetables. I serve this with almost anything, including Runner Beans with Cactus (page 146), Beer-braised Rabbit (page 153), and Rajas con Crema (page 78). It's also very common in Mexico to simply spoon the rice into a warm tortilla with slices of hard-boiled egg and salsa, a presentation known as a* taco placero. *The rice keeps in an airtight container in the refrigerator for about a week.*

1   Fill a medium saucepan two-thirds full with water and add the tomatoes. Bring to a gentle simmer over medium heat. Cook until the tomatoes have softened, 7 to 10 minutes. Transfer the tomatoes to a blender jar, reserving the cooking water for the rice. (Drain the water if you plan to use stock.)

2   Blend the tomatoes until very smooth, yielding about 1 cup tomato purée.

3   Heat the oil over medium heat in a large saucepan or medium-size clay pot, if you have one. When hot, add the rice and stir, coating it in the oil. (It may stick a little.) Add the onion and fry, stirring often, until the rice grains start to sound almost raspy, like pebbles shaking in the pan, about 10 minutes.

4   Add the tomato purée, 3 cups of the reserved tomato water or stock, and the peas and carrots. Stir in the salt, taste and add more if necessary. Top with the serrano chile.

5   Bring to a boil, then lower the heat to the lowest it will go, and cover. Cook until all the liquid has been absorbed, 12 to 15 minutes—the tomato purée should have formed a layer on top of the rice. Stir well and serve immediately.

2 plum tomatoes, or other ripe, fresh tomato
¼ cup canola oil
2 cups long-grain or extra-long-grain white rice
⅛ medium onion, chopped
3 cups Basic Homemade Chicken Stock (page 98) or water
½ cup fresh or frozen peas
1 carrot, finely chopped
1½ teaspoons salt
1 serrano chile, finely chopped

TO SOAK OR NOT TO SOAK?

In Mexico City, many cooks swear by soaking their rice in hot water before cooking, insisting it's the key step to fluffy, well-cooked rice. In the United States, this step is not necessary—if you soak the rice in hot water beforehand, it will overcook in the pot and turn sticky.

CALDO DE POLLO
BASIC HOMEMADE CHICKEN STOCK

3 pounds chicken parts, excess
    fat trimmed
½ pound chicken feet
½ medium onion, quartered,
    skin left on
2 garlic cloves, peeled

Many traditional Mexican dishes rely on homemade chicken stock for extra depth of flavor. It's essential in moles, as a base in soups, to thin out chile sauces in guisados, and when cooking rice or noodles. This is not a heavy, rich stock like you'd find in a European kitchen, and you don't need carrots or celery or parsley—just a little onion and garlic. Some Mexican cooks use chicken backs and feet to develop a gelatinous texture in the broth, and I'm a fan, too. In the U.S., you can generally find them sold cheaply at Asian supermarkets, but feel free to use necks, legs and thighs as well. This stock freezes beautifully in airtight containers or in ice cube trays.

1   Place the chicken parts and feet in a large deep pot with enough water to cover. Add the onion and garlic. Bring to a boil.

2   Skim off any foam or scum that rises to the surface, then lower the heat to medium-low and gently simmer, uncovered. Remove the thighs and drumsticks when the meat is tender, after about 25 minutes. When cool enough to handle, shred the meat and return the bones to the pot. Save the meat for another use.

3   Simmer the stock for another 2½ hours, uncovered, adding more water if necessary. Let cool.

4   Refrigerate the stock overnight. In the morning, scoop off any fat that's accumulated on the surface. Warm the stock, strain and let cool. At this point the stock is ready to use or freeze.

COOKING TIP: *If you don't have time to make this stock, you can make a very light chicken broth by poaching chicken pieces in water with 1 small garlic clove and a small wedge of onion, plus a small bay leaf and a few peppercorns. Place the ingredients in a pot and cover with 8 cups cold water. Bring to a boil, then cook over very low heat, covered, for about 30 minutes for 2½ pounds of chicken. Let cool then shred the meat. At that point the broth can be strained and used.*

Canned or packaged low-sodium chicken stocks will work in Mexican cooking most of the time, but I've found them too aggressive and rich for mole, which counts on a delicate balance of flavors, and white rice. In those cases, it's best to use homemade.

CREMA DE ELOTE
CREAMY CORN SOUP

Creamy soups are served before the rice or as an alternative to consommé on fonda *menus. They're a bit heavier than their brothy counterparts, although many don't contain cream—just puréed vegetables and stock. This version is a modification of a corn soup found in Josefina Velázquez de León's excellent bilingual cookbook,* Mexican Cook Book Devoted to American Homes, *published in 1947. Because American corn is so sweet, it doesn't exactly mirror the corn soups served in Mexico, which are starchier and heartier. But it's still flavorful, not too rich, and best served in the summer, when corn is at its peak. See page 100 for a photo of this soup with Creamy Beet Soup (page 101).*

1 Melt the butter in a large heavy pot over medium-low heat. Add the onion and garlic. Cook, stirring often, until the onion is translucent, 3 to 4 minutes. Add the corn, stock, salt and white pepper.

2 Bring to a boil, then lower the flame and simmer, covered, for about 20 minutes or until the flavors meld and the corn cooks through. Transfer the soup to a blender jar and blend until smooth, then pour it back into the pot (or use an immersion blender). The soup should still be hot.

3 Stir in the cream, taste and adjust the seasonings. Serve the soup immediately, topped with the cheese and a sprinkle of fresh chopped cilantro.

COOKING TIP: *Crumbled queso añejo would be a typical garnish here, but good-quality queso añejo can be hard to find outside Mexico. As a substitute, I like Haystack Mountain's aged queso de mano, a goat cheese available online or at specialty cheese shops.*

4 tablespoons (½ stick) unsalted butter

1 small onion, minced

2 medium garlic cloves, minced

6 ears of fresh corn, shucked, kernels cut from the cobs

1 quart Basic Homemade Chicken Stock (see opposite)

1½ teaspoons salt, or more to taste

⅛ teaspoon ground white pepper

½ cup heavy cream

½ cup grated or cubed queso de mano or queso añejo

chopped fresh cilantro

CREMA DE BETABEL
CREAMY BEET SOUP

I spied this soup on a creative comida corrida *menu a few years back, and I took a picture to remind myself to try it. When I did, the soup was no longer on the menu. This version reflects how I imagine it might have tasted: full and earthy, with a contrasting texture from toasted pumpkin seeds. The color is also gorgeous—a deep, intense pink like you'd see painted on a house in Mexico City. The soup works well as a first course to a heavier entrée, such as Purslane in Tomatillo Sauce (page 110), or as a light dinner with a vegetable-forward* guisado, *such as Stewed Swiss Chard (page 111). This soup is photographed with the Creamy Corn Soup on page 99.*

1 Preheat the oven to 400°F. If necessary, slice off and reserve the beet greens for another use. (They're great in *guisados*—see "Sweated" Mexican Greens, page 79, or Stewed Swiss Chard, page 111, for inspiration.) Wrap the beets, garlic clove, and onion tightly in aluminum foil and bake until very tender when pierced with a fork, about 1 hour and 20 minutes, depending on their size. (Unwrap every 30 minutes or so to make sure the beets are moist; if they look dry, add a tablespoon or so of water and wrap again tightly.) Let cool.

2 Reduce the oven temperature to 200°F and roast the pumpkin seeds on a sheet pan until slightly golden brown, 8 to 10 minutes. (You can also do this on the stovetop in a dry skillet.)

3 Meanwhile, place a paper towel over your hand so it doesn't stain, and then peel the beets. Cut off and discard the tops. Reserve 1 beet for garnish, if desired, dicing it into ¼-inch cubes; set aside. Chop the remaining beets coarsely and set aside.

4 Working in batches if necessary, add the coarsely chopped beets, roasted onion, and garlic to a blender jar with the milk and chicken stock, blending on high for a few minutes until smooth. Add the crema and ½ cup of the pumpkin seeds and blend again until smooth.

5 Gently heat the oil in a large saucepan or Dutch oven over medium-low heat. When hot, add the beet purée, salt, and pepper. Cook only until warmed through, 5 to 8 minutes, being careful not to scald the soup. Taste and adjust the seasonings.

6 Serve immediately, topping each bowl with the remaining toasted pumpkin seeds, beet cubes and chopped fresh cilantro. (For a little more acidity, toss the beet cubes with a few teaspoons of crema before adding to the soup.)

2 pounds beets, scrubbed free of any dirt
1 garlic clove, unpeeled
¼ medium onion
¾ cup pumpkin seeds
2½ cups whole milk
2 cups Basic Homemade Chicken Stock (page 98)
½ cup Homemade Crema, plus more for serving (page 139)
1 tablespoon olive oil
¾ teaspoon salt, or more to taste
⅛ teaspoon white pepper
fresh cilantro, chopped

SOPA SECA DE FIDEO
FIDEO NOODLES IN CHIPOTLE-TOMATO SAUCE

Another "dry soup" served before the main meal, sopa seca de fideo *is one of my favorite dishes in Mexico. Thin fried noodles mingle in a (sometimes spicy) tomato sauce, garnished with crema, avocado slices, and once, when I was lucky, big pieces of* chicharrón—*it added a crunch and meatiness I didn't even know I was missing. Not everyone adds chipotle en adobo; I like the heat and slight fruitiness it gives the sauce. This is usually served as a side dish, but can also stand up as a meal on its own. Leftovers will keep in the fridge for about a week.*

6 ripe plum tomatoes

2 tablespoons minced, canned chipotles en adobo, plus 1 teaspoon adobo sauce

½ teaspoon brown sugar or grated *piloncillo* (page 61)

2 cloves garlic, peeled

¼ medium onion

3 tablespoons canola oil

1 (12-ounce) package *fideo* noodles

½ teaspoon salt, plus more to taste

½ cup Homemade Crema (page 139)

½ ripe Haas avocado, peeled, pitted, and thinly sliced

1 scant cup crumbled queso fresco

pieces of *chicharrón* (pork cracklings), optional

1   Fill a medium saucepan two-thirds full with water and add the tomatoes. Bring to a gentle simmer over medium heat and cook until softened, 7 to 10 minutes. (If the tomatoes start to split before they've softened, lower the heat.) Transfer to a small bowl and reserve 1 cup of the cooking water.

2   In a small bowl, mix together the minced chipotle, adobo sauce, and brown sugar. Set aside.

3   Slip the skins off of the tomatoes and add them, with any juices left in the bowl, to a blender jar with the garlic, onion and ½ cup of the reserved cooking water. Blend on high until very smooth.

4   Add 1 tablespoon of the oil to a large skillet set over medium heat. When hot, fry half the noodles, stirring often so they don't burn, until they're a deep golden brown. Transfer to paper towels to drain. Wipe the pan and repeat with 1 tablespoon oil and the second batch of noodles.

5   Wipe the pan clean once more and heat the remaining tablespoon oil. When hot, pour in the tomato purée (careful, it may splatter) and fry on medium to medium-low heat, sprinkling on the salt. Cook, stirring occasionally, until the sauce no longer tastes of raw onion and garlic, 4 to 5 minutes. Mix in the chipotle paste and taste for seasoning.

6   Add the fried noodles and cook over medium-low heat until they absorb nearly all the sauce, about 5 minutes. Taste the noodles—if they're still too chewy, add the remaining ½ cup reserved cooking water and cook until all the sauce is just absorbed and the noodles are al dente.

7   Serve on individual plates, topped with crema, avocado slices, and crumbled cheese. Place *chicharrón* pieces on the side, if serving.

COOKING TIPS: Fideo *noodles are thin like angel hair pasta, and in Mexico City they come in various sizes; the most common is about 1 inch long. In the U.S., at Mexican grocery stores or in the Hispanic foods aisle of mainstream grocery stores, some are sold in bundles that can be broken into pieces. Canned chipotle en adobo can vary in acidity, depending on the brand. Make sure to taste and adjust the sugar or heat in the sauce as necessary.*

HUEVOS MONTULEÑOS
MONTULEÑO-STYLE EGGS

Originated in Yucatán, this snazzier version of huevos rancheros *(as I think of it) is served for breakfast in many Mexico City* fondas. *Corn tortillas are sandwiched together with refried beans, topped with fried eggs, a sprinkling of diced ham, cooked peas and a heavy ladleful of spicy tomato sauce. While the Yucatecan sauce may be somewhat chunky, at home I like to make this with a smooth, thick ranchera sauce. The traditional serving size is two eggs per person, but I think one is plenty, combined with all the other elements on the plate. Like a lot of Mexican breakfast dishes, this tastes best if served immediately, while the egg yolks are still runny.*

1   Prepare the ranchera sauce and the refried beans and set aside on the stove to keep warm.

2   In a large skillet, fry 2 tortillas lightly in 2 teaspoons of the lard until lightly toasted. (You don't want them too crispy.) Drain on a layer of paper towels or a wire rack set over a rimmed baking sheet. Repeat until all the tortillas have been fried. Keep warm in a gently heated oven.

3   Add ½ teaspoon lard to the same pan. When hot, add the peas and ham and season with salt and pepper to taste. Cook until just warmed through, about 2 minutes. Cover and keep warm.

4   Crack 1 egg into a small bowl. Coat the bottom of a small frying pan in lard or oil and warm over medium heat. When hot, pour in the egg, cover the pan, lower the heat slightly and cook just until the whites set, 2 to 3 minutes.

5   Meanwhile, place 2 tortillas on a plate. Smear one with a layer of refried beans, then top with the other. Carefully slide the fried egg on top. Add a generous ladle of ranchera sauce and sprinkle with peas, ham and cheese. Nestle fried plantain slices on the side, if using. Serve immediately.

6   Repeat steps 4 and 5 with the remaining eggs, tortillas, refried beans, and garnishes.

1 batch Ranchera Sauce (see opposite)
1 batch Quick Refried Beans (page 45)
8 corn tortillas
2 tablespoons lard or canola oil
1½ cups fresh or frozen peas, thawed
1 scant cup diced, thick-cut ham
salt and freshly ground black pepper
4 large eggs
1 scant cup queso fresco or queso añejo
fried plantain slices, optional

RANCHERA SAUCE

I serve this spicy, puréed tomato sauce with huevos rancheros, Fried Huauzontle Patties (page 120), or even spooned onto scrambled eggs. You can make it as thin or as thick as you like, but I like mine slightly thicker than spaghetti sauce.

1   Place the tomatoes, chiles, garlic and onion in a Dutch oven and cover with cold water. (The tomatoes will float.) Bring to medium heat, simmering gently, until the tomato flesh softens, about 8 minutes. The chile and onion may take a few minutes longer—the chile is done when the skin darkens and becomes slightly matte; the onion should be translucent.

2   Drain and transfer the tomato mixture to a bowl, reserving ¼ cup of the cooking water. Let cool to room temperature.

3   Stem the chiles and chop roughly. Place them in a blender jar with the onion and garlic. Slip off and discard the tomato skins, add the tomatoes to the blender jar and blend until smooth. (You may need to do this in batches, depending on the power of your blender). If the sauce seems very thick, add the reserved cooking water and blend again until smooth.

4   Heat the lard in a large skillet over medium heat. When it melts, add the sauce in one quick pour. (Be careful—it might splatter.) Season with the salt, or more to taste. Bring to a boil, then lower the heat and simmer gently until the flavors meld, stirring occasionally, about 5 minutes. Keep warm if using immediately.

2 pounds plum tomatoes
2 medium serrano chiles
1 large garlic clove, peeled
¼ medium onion
1 tablespoon lard or canola oil
¾ teaspoon salt

HUEVO CON FRIJOL
BEANS AND EGGS

Eating beans and eggs together is nothing new in Mexican cooking, but serving them in a fluffy, cylindrical shape is something I'd never seen before until I sat down for breakfast at Fonda La Indita in the Centro. The tiny, windowless spot looks like it hasn't changed in at least a hundred years—exposed wooden beams still line the tall ceilings, and a woman near the door still makes homemade corn tortillas from an old-fashioned conveyor-belt tortilla press.

A few months later, curious about this presentation, I went back and owner Amparo Reina Rendón kindly invited me into the kitchen. There, a cook mashed together beans and eggs, placed them in an oiled frying pan and jerked the pan forward and back. The mix slid up the side of the pan and flipped over into a perfect cylindrical roll. To eat, tear off a piece of warm corn tortilla, pinch off a bit of beans and eggs and spoon salsa on top.

4 cups Basic Cooked Beans
    (see opposite), with ¼ cup
    bean broth
8 teaspoons canola oil
8 large eggs
salt
8 corn tortillas
salsa of choice

COOKING TIP: *You need a small, well-oiled (or nonstick) frying pan to make sure the flip works correctly. The cylindrical shape doesn't affect the flavor, though, so if you can't get the hang of it, just serve them normally. For smaller portions, try ½ cup beans, 1 teaspoon bean broth, and 1 egg per person.*

1   Measure out 1 cup beans and 1 tablespoon broth into a small bowl. Mash lightly until coarsely textured. There should be some half-mashed beans and some beans left whole. Set aside.

2   Warm 1 teaspoon of the oil in a medium frying pan on medium-high heat. Crack 2 eggs into a small bowl and beat them lightly.

3   Once the pan is hot, add the eggs and stir quickly, sprinkling on a pinch of salt. Keep stirring until the eggs are just cooked through, about 30 seconds.

4   Add the cooked eggs to the mashed beans and mash together with a flat instrument—I like using the bottom of a heatproof cup—until the mixture becomes a thick, evenly combined mass. Taste and season with more salt if needed.

5   Wipe down the frying pan and heat again to medium-high heat. Add another teaspoon oil. When hot, add the bean and egg mixture, shaking the pan slightly to even out the mass. Cook for 15 to 20 seconds, stir, and shake to even out again. Cook for another 20 to 30 seconds, until warmed through.

6   To flip, pick up the frying pan by the handle and gently but quickly flick it back, slightly up, and then toward you. The mixture should slide to the back of the pan, inch up the side with the momentum, and then flip over into a torpedo shape. (If you've made a French omelet before, it's a similar motion.)

7   Remove carefully to an ovenproof plate and place in a gently heated oven. Repeat steps 1 through 6 three times. Serve immediately with warm corn tortillas and salsa.

FRIJOLES BÁSICOS
BASIC COOKED BEANS

For years I wondered how to make stewed beans like the ones I'd enjoyed in the fondas. They were so simple and perfect, I didn't think an unskilled hand could succeed. It turns out two factors make the biggest difference: the quality of the beans and the amount of liquid you cook them in. Soaking them, a practice roundly embraced in Mexico City, isn't always necessary, although they will take longer to cook if not. These go with almost anything: eggs, spooned into a tortilla, as a side dish for nearly any guisado, mashed and smeared onto a tostada, or served warm and sprinkled with your favorite cheese.

1   The day before you wish to eat them, pick over the beans and remove any stones or foreign matter. Place in a large bowl, cover with cold water and soak overnight. (Alternatively, skip the soaking if you prefer.)

2   Drain the beans and cover with 2 inches fresh cold water (3 inches if unsoaked) and bring to a boil. Lower the heat to medium, add the epazote if using, and simmer for 45 to 60 minutes, stirring occasionally, until the beans are tender and the innards creamy and smooth. (Unsoaked beans may take an additional 45 minutes to cook.) About 5 to 10 minutes before—when the beans are mostly soft, but not quite silky—add salt to taste. You can now eat the beans as is, or continue on.

3   Transfer the beans and broth to a bowl. Heat the lard in the same pot over medium. When hot, add the garlic and onion and cook, stirring constantly, until blistered and dark golden.

4   Add the beans and broth in one swift pour (careful, it may splatter). Bring to a boil, taste and adjust the seasonings. Serve immediately.

VARIATION: *To create a richer, thicker bean broth, remove 1 cup beans and 1 cup cooking liquid to a separate bowl once the beans are done cooking. Mash together, just enough to release the bean starches into the broth (the beans should have a rustic texture). Strain and add the starchy broth back to the pot, or, if you don't mind small bits of mashed bean in your pot, add the whole thing. Continue cooking until warmed through.*

COOKING TIP: *Don't drown the beans in water at the beginning—the concentrated cooking liquid left at the end is almost as important as the beans themselves. Unsoaked beans might need perhaps 3 inches of water to cover; soaked beans a little less. At higher altitudes, you'll need a pressure cooker or a kettle filled with warm water, to replenish as necessary. (Don't use cold water or the beans may come out half-cooked.)*

I stew—"guisar"—these beans after cooking them, meaning I fry them in a little lard, onion and garlic. This step adds a lot of flavor, but you can skip it or do it later if you're running short on time. In Mexico City, most cooked beans typically include epazote, which adds a subtle herbal bitterness. If you can't find it, leave it out.

Bean cooking times can vary, depending on altitude and how old the beans are. Aim for creamy, silky innards.

1 pound dried beans, such as
   pinto or black
3 to 5 sprigs epazote, optional
salt
2 tablespoons lard or canola oil
1 medium garlic clove, peeled
¼ medium onion, chopped

MOLE DE OLLA
MOLE FROM THE POT

Not all Mexican moles are thick sauces ladled over meat. This one, popular in fondas and at homes across Central Mexico, is a soup. The dish starts with a full-bodied, chile-accented beef broth, combined with chunks of stewed beef, corn on the cob, squash and green beans, traditionally eaten as a midday meal. The base of my version comes from my friend Janneth López, whom I met in cooking school. It calls for a bit more time and labor than other mole de olla recipes, but the result is a warm, rich broth that's so good you'll want to drink it plain, assuming you can handle the kick. This freezes beautifully.

For the meat:

2 pounds beef chuck or short ribs, cut into large pieces

1 pound veal or marrow bones

¼ large onion

2 cloves garlic, peeled

2 stems fresh thyme

5 peppercorns

1 celery stalk, roughly chopped

1 carrot, roughly chopped

For the sauce:

8 costeño chiles (see Tip)

2 guajillo chiles

2 pasilla chiles

1 tablespoon canola oil, plus more for frying

4 peppercorns

2 cloves

½ teaspoon anise seed

½ teaspoon Mexican oregano

2 heaping teaspoons minced fresh ginger

scant ½ teaspoon ground nutmeg

2 plum tomatoes, quartered

4 small cloves garlic, peeled

⅛ medium onion

salt

2 teaspoons lard or canola oil

2 ears of corn, husked and cut into four pieces each

4 ounces green beans, sliced into 2-inch lengths

1 chayote, unpeeled, sliced pole to pole and thinly sliced

1 large Mexican squash, cut into ½-inch-thick half-moons

5 to 8 stems epazote, or to taste

12 corn tortillas

4 limes, cut into wedges

COOKING TIP: *In Mexico, dried costeño chiles are short, red or yellow, and quite hot. In the U.S., they are squat, plump, and not as hot. If you find the real ones, start with five, or use chile puya, a type of hotter guajillo, or regular chile guajillos.*

1   To prepare the meat, place all of the ingredients in a large deep pot and cover with cold water. Bring to a boil and skim off any scum that floats to the surface. Reduce the heat to low and simmer gently, partially covered, until tender, about 1 hour 45 minutes. Transfer the meat to a bowl and strain the broth, discarding the aromatics. Skim off any large pools of fat. Reserve ½ cup broth for the sauce. At this point you can refrigerate the meat and remaining broth for up to 2 days.

2   To make the sauce, snip the stems off the dried chiles and shake out the seeds. (If they're too brittle, toast them first on a *comal* to soften.) Coat a small frying pan with the oil and warm to medium heat. Add the chiles in batches, frying one variety at a time and stirring constantly, until they change color and emit a spicy aroma, about 10 seconds. Be careful not to burn them. Set aside.

3   Grind the peppercorns, cloves and anise seed in a mortar. Transfer to a blender jar with the oregano, ginger, nutmeg, tomatoes, ½ cup reserved broth, garlic, onion, fried chiles and a pinch of salt. Blend on high until smooth.

4   Heat the lard in a medium frying pan over medium heat. Add the chile sauce in one quick pour (stand back as it may splatter). Cook until it darkens, stirring often so the bottom doesn't stick, 8 to 10 minutes.

5   Bring the broth and meat to a gentle simmer in a large deep pot. Pour in the chile sauce and add the corn, green beans and 1 tablespoon salt. Bring to a boil, then reduce the heat to low and simmer until the beans are almost tender, 15 to 20 minutes. Add the chayote, squash, and epazote and cook for 10 minutes or until the squash is tender. Taste and add more salt or epazote if desired—the herb should taste noticeable.

6   Serve the soup in large deep bowls. Warm the tortillas and pass them at the table in a basket or wrapped in a cloth, along with the lime wedges.

VERDOLAGAS EN SALSA VERDE
PURSLANE IN TOMATILLO SAUCE

2½ pounds pork backbones or pork ribs,
    cut into large pieces
¼ medium onion
1 large garlic clove
salt

For the sauce:
2 pounds tomatillos, husked and rinsed
2 large serrano chiles
2 medium garlic cloves, peeled
1 small onion, cut in half
2 teaspoons lard or canola oil
salt
2 pounds purslane, ends trimmed
2 heaping tablespoons coarsely chopped
    fresh cilantro, or more to taste
1 batch Basic Cooked Beans (page 107)
8 to 12 corn tortillas, warmed

Purslane, known as verdolagas *in Spanish, is usually served cooked in Mexico City, although some upscale restaurants have recently started to embrace its use in salads. Stewing the greens in tomatillo sauce—often in a clay pot—is a classic preparation: earthy and lightly acidic, with a pleasing al dente texture. Corn tortillas and beans are usually the only accompaniments.*

1   Rinse the pork and place in a large pot. Cover with cold water and add the onion and garlic. Bring to a boil and add a few hefty pinches of salt. Skim off any scum that accumulates on the surface. Lower the heat to medium-low, cover and simmer gently until the meat is extremely tender when pierced with a fork, about 2 hours. Remove 2 cups of the broth from the pot and set aside. Let the meat sit in the pot while you make the sauce.

2   Fill a medium saucepan two-thirds full with water and bring to a slow, rolling boil. Add the tomatillos, serranos, garlic, and onion and boil until the tomatillos and chiles have softened and turned a dull green color, 8 to 10 minutes. Strain and transfer to a blender jar with 1 cup of the reserved broth. Blend on high until smooth.

3   Heat the lard over medium heat in a large deep pan or Dutch oven. When hot, add the tomatillo sauce in one quick pour and fry for a few minutes, seasoning with salt. Add the meat and bring to a boil. (Add the additional cup of reserved pork broth if you'd like a thinner texture.) Lower the heat to medium and cook until the flavors meld, 5 to 8 minutes. Add the purslane and cook for 5 minutes more, partially covered, until limp and tender. Stir in the cilantro.

4   To serve, spoon the pork, greens and sauce onto individual plates, giving each a side of beans. Pass warm corn tortillas at the table.

COOKING TIP: *Tomatillos vary in acidity. The sauce should be acidic, but not mouth-puckeringly so. If yours are too tart, add more onion to the blender.*

If you can't find pork backbones, a cheaper cut known as espinazo *in Spanish, try pork ribs. Vegetarians can also leave out the meat and lard and increase the veggies, and use the tomatillo cooking water or vegetable stock in lieu of pork broth.*

GUISADO DE ACELGAS
STEWED SWISS CHARD

Chard is available year-round in Mexico City, and it's most commonly consumed stewed in a mix of chile, onion, garlic and perhaps tomatoes. There's no exact ratio that works best—the ideal dish should be simple and comforting. I've added garbanzo beans here after seeing the idea in an out-of-print Mexican cookbook; they add a creaminess to the dish that I like. You can add a minced serrano chile, too, for a touch of heat. Nothing else is needed but corn tortillas, salsa, and a little avocado.

1   Heat the oil in a Dutch oven over medium-high heat. Add the onion and garlic and cook until softened and translucent, about 3 minutes.

2   Lower the heat to medium. Add the tomatoes and chard stems and sprinkle with salt. Cook until the tomatoes start to break down and soften, 3 to 4 minutes.

3   Stir in the garbanzo beans and chicken stock. Then add the chard leaves in batches, tossing together with tongs until wilted. Sprinkle with more salt, lower the heat, cover and cook until the leaves soften and the stems are tender, 5 to 8 minutes. Taste and adjust seasonings, and then transfer to a serving bowl.

4   Serve with warm corn tortillas, sliced avocado, lime wedges and salsa, so guests can make their own tacos.

3 teaspoons canola oil
½ cup chopped onion
2 cloves garlic, minced
2 plum tomatoes, chopped
2 large bunches chard, stems diced and
    leaves torn into small pieces
salt
1 cup cooked garbanzo beans, or
    1 (15-ounce) can, drained and rinsed
¼ cup Basic Homemade Chicken Stock
    (page 98), vegetable stock, or water
12 corn tortillas, warmed
1 ripe Haas avocado, peeled, pitted, and
    thinly sliced
3 limes, cut into wedges
salsa of choice

STEAK IN CHILE PASILLA SAUCE

This guisado is popular across Central Mexico, and you'll often see it in fondas, simmering away in a clay pot. Thin pieces of steak, cooked until tender, are added to a seasoned chile pasilla sauce that is so good it's nearly impossible not to sop up every bit with a rolled-up tortilla. Lightly fried potatoes on the side add a good, starchy counterpoint. (And another reason to slather your plate with sauce.)

3 large waxy potatoes, scrubbed

7 pasilla chiles, seeds and veins removed, and toasted briefly on a *comal*

10 ounces tomatillos

1 small onion, cut into quarters or thickly sliced

1 garlic clove, unpeeled

1½ cups Basic Homemade Chicken Stock (page 98), beef broth, or both mixed with a little chile water

2 pounds beef steaks, sliced very thinly and cut into 2-inch pieces

salt and freshly ground black pepper

2 tablespoons plus 2 teaspoons lard or canola oil

12 corn tortillas, warmed on a *comal*

1   Place the potatoes in a large saucepan and cover with cold water. Bring to a boil, then lower the heat to medium-high and simmer for about 20 minutes, until just tender when pierced with a fork. Place the chiles in a bowl of warm water and let sit until their skins soften, 15 to 20 minutes. (Reserve the soaking water if you'd like to use it as flavoring later.)

2   Meanwhile, place the tomatillos, onion, and garlic on a *comal* or nonstick skillet over medium heat. Cook, turning occasionally, until blackened in spots and the garlic turns a bit squishy, 10 to 12 minutes. Peel the garlic and place in a blender jar with the tomatillos, onion, softened chiles and 1 cup of the stock or broth. Blend on high until very smooth and set aside. Strain the potatoes and cut into any shape you want (I like half-moons) and set aside.

3   Season the steaks well with salt and pepper. In a large saucepan or Dutch oven, warm 2 tablespoons lard over high heat. Add the steaks and cook, flipping once, until the meat turns juicy and darkens in color and the fat foams then subsides, 6 to 8 minutes.

4   Add the sauce in one quick pour, plus ½ cup of the reserved chile water, stock or broth. Stir well, then turn to very low heat, cover and simmer for about 20 minutes, until the flavors meld and the meat softens a bit. Season with more salt.

5   Meanwhile, heat the remaining 2 teaspoons lard in a large skillet over medium-high heat. Add the potatoes in an even layer and sprinkle with a hefty pinch of salt. Let sit undisturbed for 4 to 5 minutes, then turn over and cook the other side—they should have a nice golden-brown crust. Sprinkle with more salt, lower the heat and cover, stirring occasionally, until crispy on the outside and soft in the middle, 15 to 20 minutes.

6   Serve immediately, transferring the meat to a large bowl in the middle of the table and letting guests help themselves. Pass the potatoes and warm corn tortillas.

COOKING TIP: *In Mexico, you can ask the butcher for "steak for making* bistec en salsa de pasilla*" and he'll know exactly what you mean. In the U.S. and elsewhere, look for a cut without too much connective tissue—the meat simmers for less than a half hour in the sauce, so it doesn't have a lot of time to break down and soften. Ideally a butcher will slice the steaks for you; the thinner the slices, the faster they will cook in the sauce.*

ALBONDIGAS AL CHIPOTLE
MEATBALLS IN CHIPOTLE SAUCE

In Central Mexico, meatballs in chipotle sauce are a thick, nourishing dish, served as the main midday meal. Inside the large meatballs you often get a little surprise: a piece of cooked egg. This recipe comes from my friend Nick Zukin, a cook and author who owns the Mi Mero Mole taquerias in Portland, Oregon, which specialize in guisados from Mexico City. While fondas in Mexico would generally serve two or three of these large meatballs on a plate, smothered in sauce, Nick's favorite way to eat them is in a torta with stringy, melted quesillo cheese. The only accompaniments you need here are warm corn tortillas, beans and rice—or a roll and cheese if you go Nick's route.

1   To make the meatballs, mix together the beef, pork, ham, breadcrumbs, salt, and pepper. (This works best with your hands.) Mix in the milk and beaten egg until thoroughly combined. Divide into 24 (2-tablespoon) portions. Form each into a patty and place a piece of chopped boiled egg in the center, then wrap the patty around the egg and make sure to close any seams tightly. Roll into a ball. Set aside.

2   To make the sauce, heat 1 tablespoon of the lard in a Dutch oven or large saucepan over medium heat. When hot, add the onion and garlic and cook until translucent and soft, 3 minutes. Transfer to a blender jar with the tomatoes, chipotles and chicken stock and blend on high until very smooth. Add the salt and refrigerate the sauce for up to 24 hours if you're not ready to use it. To reheat, add 2 teaspoons lard to the same pot and add the sauce when the lard is hot.

3   Bring the sauce to a boil and add the meatballs, making sure not to break them. Shake the pot a bit to settle the meatballs fully into the sauce. Return to a boil and lower the heat to medium or medium-low, simmering gently, covered, for 1 hour or until fully cooked.

4   To serve, warm the corn tortillas on a *comal* or in the microwave and place them in a basket or cloth. Ladle meatballs and heavy spoonfuls of the sauce onto individual plates, making sure the meatballs are completely covered with sauce. Spoon a side of rice and beans onto each plate. Pass the warm tortillas at the table.

COOKING TIP: *Unless you can find excellent ripe tomatoes, I'd recommend using canned tomatoes for this dish, which are actually more flavorful than the bland tomatoes found year-round in most parts of the United States. The sauce can be prepared ahead of time, and any extra sauce works well drizzled over eggs or pasta.*

For the meatballs:

8 ounces ground beef

8 ounces ground pork

4 ounces finely chopped ham steak

½ cup breadcrumbs (1 slice of white bread, toasted and pulsed in a food processor)

1 teaspoon salt

¼ teaspoon ground black pepper

¼ cup whole milk

1 large egg, lightly beaten

2 large eggs, hard-boiled, each chopped into 12 equal pieces

For the sauce:

1 tablespoon lard or canola oil, plus more for frying

½ large onion, chopped

1 garlic clove, roughly chopped

3 (14.5-ounce) cans fire-roasted tomatoes, drained

3 canned chipotles en adobo (use less if you want less heat)

½ cup Basic Homemade Chicken Stock (page 98)

1½ teaspoons salt, or more to taste

18 corn tortillas

1 batch Mexican-Style Red Rice (page 97)

1 batch Basic Cooked Beans (page 107)

TACOS DORADOS DE ZANAHORIA
CRISPY CARROT TACOS

Tacos dorados in Mexico City are what I grew up knowing as taquitos: rolled tubes of corn tortillas, stuffed with some sort of meat and fried until crisp. At fondas in the capital, they're generally served three or four to a plate and covered in crema, crumbly cheese and lettuce. Most fondas will prepare at least one vegetarian dish on their comida corrida menu, but it still surprised me to see carrot tacos at my friend Miguel Garduño's tiny eatery in Azcapotzalco. One bite revealed a crispy exterior and steamy, salty shredded carrot innards, so plain and pretty that I couldn't help wanting to make them at home. They're deceptively easy and don't need much beyond raw carrots and salt. I pan-fry these instead of deep frying, and I like lots of acid (lime juice and tomatillo salsa) and beans on the side. You'll also need toothpicks to secure them closed while cooking.

1   Heat the oven to 200°F and line a baking sheet with a wire rack, or several layers of paper towels.

2   In a mixing bowl, toss the grated carrot with the salt.

3   Warm the corn tortillas on a *comal* or in the microwave and place in a dishcloth to keep warm.

4   Place one tortilla on a work surface. Using your hands or tongs, place a small handful of carrot in the center, taking care not to spread the filling all the way to the edge. Roll the tortilla tightly around the filling and secure closed with a toothpick. Repeat until you've got 12 tacos.

5   Heat the oil over medium heat in a large frying pan. Add the tacos seam-side down and cook until they start to smell toasty, 2 to 3 minutes. Turn over and fry on the other side until golden. (If you're a perfectionist like me, you can also roll them around a bit with tongs to make sure they're fried evenly on all sides.) Transfer to the prepared baking sheet, then keep warm in the oven. Repeat until all the tacos have been fried.

6   To serve, place 3 tacos on a plate, slather with a layer of crema and top with crumbled cheese. Pass lime wedges and tomatillo salsa at the table

5 cups grated carrot (about 3 large carrots)
½ teaspoon salt
12 corn tortillas
¼ cup canola oil, plus more if needed
1 (16-ounce) container Mexican crema (or make your own, page 139)
1 (14-ounce) package queso fresco, or any other creamy, crumbled cheese
3 to 4 limes, cut into wedges
1 batch Raw Tomatillo Salsa (page 26)

ENCHILADAS POTOSINAS
CHEESY ENCHILADA POCKETS.

These enchiladas, made from tortillas infused with guajillo chile sauce, are native to San Luis Potosí, a capital city located about five hours north of the Federal District by bus. While they're not extremely common in Mexico City, you can find them at the occasional fonda or market food stall, lightly fried and topped with spoonfuls of crema and salsa. To me they resemble quesadillas more than enchiladas. In either case, they're firecrackers: a bold tortilla pocket wrapped around a crumbly, spicy filling.

You'll need a tortilla press for this, and plastic sheets (such as those cut from a grocery bag) for lining the plates. It's also helpful to have a friend assisting with the stuffing or cooking, to help things move faster. You can freeze these after cooking on the comal, *then thaw and fry to reheat.*

3 guajillo chiles, toasted lightly on a *comal*, stems and seeds removed

1 garlic clove, unpeeled, toasted on a *comal* until soft

salt

1 pound fresh tortilla masa

2 teaspoons lard or canola oil, plus 1 to 2 tablespoons for frying

3 plum tomatoes, cored, seeded, and diced

1 large jalapeño, seeded and minced

1 heaping cup crumbled queso fresco

1 (16-ounce) container Mexican crema (or make your own, page 139)

salsa of choice

1 Place the chiles in a bowl of warm water and let sit until the skins soften, about 20 minutes. Strain and reserve the soaking liquid.

2 Peel the garlic clove and place in a blender jar with the softened chiles and about 3 tablespoons of the reserved chile water (just enough so the blades move easily). Blend until very smooth—the sauce should not be too thin. Add ½ teaspoon salt and blend again. Taste and adjust the seasonings. Set aside.

3 Knead the masa for about 1 minute if it looks dry and cracked. Add the chile sauce and knead until the sauce is completely integrated and the masa has an even orangey red color. It will be sticky (if it's a humid day, it could be even stickier). Let rest, uncovered, for 10 minutes.

4 Heat 2 teaspoons of the lard in a medium skillet over medium heat. Add the tomatoes and jalapeño and cook just until the tomatoes soften, about 2 minutes. (Don't overcook the tomatoes or they'll become too watery, making the tortillas soggy later.) Remove the pan from the heat. Stir in the cheese, season with salt and stir again.

5 Heat a *comal* or nonstick skillet to medium or slightly medium-low heat. Form the tortilla dough into 16 balls, roughly the size of golf balls.

6 Open the tortilla press and line both plates with plastic sheets. Place one tortilla ball on the bottom half of the press and flatten it slightly with your hand. Lower the top plate and push on the lever.

7 With lightly dampened hands, open the press, carefully peel off the top plastic sheet and flip the tortilla onto your open palm. Gently peel back the second layer of plastic and, sweeping your hand from left to right, or right to left, drape the tortilla across the hot *comal*. (See "Making Corn Tortillas" on page 23 for detailed instructions.)

8 Cook the tortilla for about 25 seconds or until the outer edges start to darken and crisp. Flip and cook about 10 seconds more—the tortilla should have some brown freckles, as well as a few patches that look shiny-red and raw. If it's not browned at all, turn up the heat a little and keep cooking.

9 Transfer the half-cooked tortilla to your workspace. Add about 1 tablespoon filling to one half of the tortilla, fold over and press the sides closed with your fingertips—they should smoosh together easily. If the tortilla cracks along the seam when you fold it, it hasn't been cooked long enough. (It's still edible, but make a note for the next one.) Conversely, if the edges aren't doughy enough to pinch closed, you've cooked it too long.

10 Return the enchilada to the *comal*, turning occasionally and moving to the outer edges of the pan, away from direct heat as it cooks, about 45 seconds on each side until no longer raw in the middle. You may want to cut this first one open to test if it's fully cooked in the middle. Finish forming and cooking the remaining enchiladas.

11 Heat 1 tablespoon lard in a large skillet over medium heat. Add 4 enchiladas (or less, depending on how large your pan is) and fry, cooking about 2 minutes per side until golden brown. They taste best served immediately. Repeat, frying the remaining enchiladas, adding more lard to the pan as needed. Pass the crema and salsa at the table, for guests to spoon on top.

COOKING TIPS: *If you're new to making tortillas from scratch, or even new to working with stickier masa, it may take you a few tries to get this right. Watch the tortilla carefully as it cooks—if you overcook it, or overstuff it, the seams won't pinch closed. (This is not the end of the world, as they'll still taste good.)*

I don't recommend substituting masa harina for fresh tortilla masa here. The flour will not absorb the liquid correctly, and the masa will taste crumbly and weird. Take off your rings and don't wear your best clothes as the guajillo paste stains.

CHILES RELLENOS DE FRIJOL Y QUESO
ANCHO CHILES STUFFED WITH BEANS AND CHEESE

Stuffed chiles, their stems peeking out from a layer of crisp, fried egg batter, are an iconic main course served at almost every fonda in the city, every day. There are countless ways to prepare them—with poblano chiles, with ancho chiles, with meaty picadillo filling, or even stuffed with seafood—but the simplest and best preparation in my opinion, are ancho chiles stuffed with a plain, spongy Mexican cheese, served with a thin tomato caldillo, or tomato broth, on top.

I've had trouble finding good-quality Mexican cheese outside Mexico, so here I've mixed refried black beans with fingers of queso fresco, which makes the chile more plump and filling. I've morphed the traditional caldillo—which can taste bland if you don't have excellent tomatoes—into a roasted tomato sauce. Feel free to use canned fire-roasted tomatoes if you can't find any fresh. You still get all the effects of the fonda classic: a golden chile sitting under a pool of sauce, ready to be sopped up with tortillas.

4 ancho chiles, toasted briefly on a *comal*

6 plum tomatoes

¼ medium onion

1 garlic clove, unpeeled

2 teaspoons lard

salt

2 stems fresh cilantro, chopped

1 batch Quick Refried Beans (page 45)

4 pieces of queso fresco, cut into long lengths roughly the size of your chiles

1 batch Basic Cooked Beans (page 107)

1 tablespoon plus 1 teaspoon flour

4 large eggs, separated

⅓ cup canola oil, plus more as needed

8 corn tortillas, warmed

1 (16-ounce) container Mexican crema (or make your own, page 139)

COOKING TIP: *If you're selecting chiles from a prepackaged bag, choose four that are more or less the same size.*

1   Place the chiles on a workspace and carefully make an incision into each, leaving 1 inch of space at both ends and slicing from pole to pole. As gently as possible, using a small spoon or your fingers, scrape out the seeds, making sure the chiles do not tear and that the stem stays intact. (The stem is for aesthetic purposes and nothing more. But it will look cool in the end.) Place the chiles in a bowl of warm water and let sit until their skins soften, 15 to 20 minutes, reserving the soaking water.

2   Meanwhile, heat a *comal* over medium heat. Add the tomatoes, onion and garlic. Cook, turning often, until softened and blackened in spots, 7 to 10 minutes. Set aside to cool.

3   Peel the garlic and place in a blender jar with the charred tomatoes, onion and any associated juices. Blend on high until smooth. Add ¼ cup of the chile water and blend until combined.

4   Heat the lard in a medium saucepan over medium heat. Add the sauce in one quick pour, plus salt to taste. If you like a thinner texture, add more chile water, and more salt as needed. Add the cilantro stems, bring the sauce to a boil, then lower the heat to medium or medium-low, and simmer until the flavors meld, about 5 minutes. Cover and keep warm.

5   Gently remove the chiles from their bath and pat dry with paper towels. Fill each chile with about ¼ cup refried beans, depending on their size. They should look plump. Nestle a piece of cheese inside, add some of the cooked beans mixture and push the seams closed.

6   Line a baking sheet with paper towels or a wire rack. Place 1 tablespoon flour on a plate. Roll the chiles in the flour and brush off excess. Set aside.

7   Beat the egg whites until stiff peaks form. Stir in the egg yolks one by one, mixing well after each addition. Stir in the remaining 1 teaspoon flour and ½ teaspoon salt.

8   Heat the oil in a large skillet over high heat. To test to see if the oil is ready (it must be hot enough, or else the chiles will turn soggy and taste greasy), drop a dime-size piece of batter in the oil—if it sizzles and turns golden brown within 20 seconds, it's done. Conversely, if the batter turns dark brown almost immediately, the oil is too hot and the heat must be lowered.

9   Place the bowl of batter near the stove. Holding a chile by its stem, dunk it gently into the egg batter, slathering the batter lightly on all sides. Place the chile carefully in the hot oil (the batter should puff up like a cloud). Using a spoon or spatula, bathe the chile in the hot oil until the edges start to brown, 20 to 45 seconds. Carefully flip over and brown the other side. Transfer to the prepared baking sheet and fry the remaining chiles. Keep finished chiles warm in a gently heated oven.

10   To serve, place one chile in the center of a plate. Ladle the roasted tomato sauce on top and some cooked beans on the side. Pass the warm corn tortillas and the crema at the table.

TORTITAS DE HUAUZONTLE
FRIED HUAUZONTLE PATTIES

The huauzontle is a tall, bushy vegetable in the goosefoot family. They take a fairly long time to clean, but I think they're worth the effort—the fluffy, spongy texture is unlike any American vegetable, and the taste is intensely green, like a cross between broccoli and chard. In Central Mexico, the soft, unseeded buds are scraped off the stalk, boiled, and shaped into fried patties known as tortitas. Fondas *serve the patties as a midday main course, doused in a pool of homemade tomato sauce with beans and warm tortillas on the side.*

salt and freshly ground black pepper
2 large bunches huauzontles (about 1½ pounds), cleaned (see page 171)
1 batch Ranchera Sauce (page 105)
1 tablespoon plus 1 teaspoon flour
4 large eggs, separated
¼ cup canola oil, plus more for frying
12 corn tortillas
1 batch Basic Cooked Beans (page 107)

1 Fill a large saucepan two-thirds full with cold water. Bring to a vigorous boil and add a hefty pinch of salt. Add the huauzontles and lower the heat to medium. Simmer for about 10 minutes, until tender and soft, and darker in color. Strain and set aside while you prepare the ranchera sauce. Cover the sauce and keep warm.

2 Gather the huauzontles together with your hands and squeeze together firmly, draining out any excess water. Keep squeezing until mostly dry and slightly crumbly. (This is important—if the huazontles are soggy, they will not come together and form a patty, and they'll taste rather limp.) Season with salt and pepper, tossing to combine.

3 Sprinkle 1 tablespoon flour onto a plate. Separate the huauzontles into 4 equal piles. Grab one and press tightly together, forming a patty. Repeat with the remaining huauzontles. Dust each patty lightly in flour and set aside.

4 Beat the egg whites until stiff peaks form, or when you turn the bowl upside down, the whites stay in place (in Spanish this is called *a punto de turrón*). Slowly integrate the egg yolks one by one, then add the remaining teaspoon flour and ½ teaspoon salt.

5 Pour at least ¼ inch oil in a large skillet and heat over high. The oil must be hot enough for the patties to fry correctly. To test it, place a dime-size dab of the batter in the skillet. If it sizzles and turns golden brown within 20 seconds, it's ready. If it immediately turns dark brown or golden, the oil is too hot; lower the heat.

6 Place the bowl of egg batter near the stove. Nearby set a wire rack over a baking sheet, or a plate covered with layers of paper towels.

7 Take one patty, scoop it into the egg batter, then place in the hot pan. Place a dab of egg batter on the patty to cover the bare spot where your fingers were. Use a small spoon to bathe the patty in the hot oil for about 30 seconds (this cooks the top side so you can flip with ease), then flip and cook the other side. Once the patty is golden brown all over, transfer to the prepared pan to drain.

8 These are best eaten immediately. To serve, warm the corn tortillas and place in a cloth or basket. Place one patty on a plate and ladle on a heavy spoonful of ranchera sauce. Spoon a serving of beans on the side, and pass the warm tortillas at the table.

COCHINITA PIBIL
SLOW-COOKED CITRUSY PORK

Cochinita pibil isn't native to Mexico City, but it's become part of the city's culinary cannon. A hefty pork roast is marinated in annatto seed (achiote), aromatic spices and sour orange juice, then wrapped in banana leaves and baked. The pork, tender from so many hours of cooking, ends up citrusy, tangy and just the slightest bit sweet. In Yucatán, where the dish is native, the pork is traditionally smoked in a pib, or earthen oven. Mexico City cooks often make a guisado, meaning the meat is cooked first without the marinade and then added to the citrusy sauce. I like it this way, because the sauce infuses the entire dish. The required toppings, as you make your taco, are pickled red onions and habanero salsa.

1 Preheat the oven to 300°F. Season the pork roast generously with salt and pepper.

2 If using frozen banana leaves, unwrap them and gently remove the individual leaves, one at a time. To soften the leaves—an essential step so they'll fold tightly over the roast and not tear—heat a gas burner to medium. Run the leaves lightly over the flame until the skin darkens, softens and emits a lovely perfume, 3 to 5 seconds. Make sure you move and angle the leaves so the heat hits every part of the skin.

3 Lay a leaf on a workspace. Take another leaf and lay it on top, in a cross formation. (If your leaves have tears, lay them one on top of the other to make them longer.) Place the roast in the center of the cross. Pick up the ends of the leaves and wrap the meat like a package. Place in a large Dutch oven and cover tightly with a layer of aluminum foil. Cover and bake for 3½ to 4 hours, until the meat is falling off the bone or the internal temperature reads 190°F. Cool to room temperature, then cut into medium chunks.

4 Heat a *comal* to medium or medium-low heat and, when hot, add the garlic cloves. Cook, turning occasionally, until soft and slightly squishy, 5 to 7 minutes. Transfer to a bowl and let cool. Peel the garlic once cool enough to handle.

5 Crumble the achiote paste into a blender jar. Add the sour orange juice, garlic, cumin seeds, peppercorns, allspice berries, and cinnamon and blend until smooth.

6 Heat the lard in a large deep pot over medium heat. (Don't burn it or it will give the sauce an off flavor.) Add the sauce and fry for 2 to 3 minutes, stirring constantly so it doesn't burn. Stir in 3 cups broth and the orange juice, and season lightly with salt. Simmer for 35 minutes, uncovered, to allow the juice to reduce a bit.

7 Add the meat to the pot and stir to make sure it's evenly coated in the sauce. Simmer for another 20 minutes, uncovered, on medium heat, stirring occasionally and adding more broth if it looks too dry. Stir in 1½ teaspoons salt or to taste.

8 Warm the tortillas on a *comal* and place in a cloth or basket. Serve the *cochinita pibil* in individual warm corn tortillas, or in a covered serving bowl at the table. Pass the pickled onions and salsa, so everyone can make their own taco.

5 pounds bone-in pork shoulder, with fat and skin intact

salt and freshly ground black pepper

2 long fresh banana leaves, or 1 (16-ounce) package frozen banana leaves, thawed

1 head garlic cloves, unpeeled

1 (3½-ounce) bar of achiote paste (I like El Yucateco or Marin brands)

1 cup sour orange juice (about 7 oranges), or Sour Orange Substitute (page 123)

1 teaspoon cumin seeds, toasted

½ teaspoon peppercorns

3 allspice berries

1 (2-inch) cinnamon stick, toasted

1 teaspoon lard or canola oil

3 to 4 cups pork broth or Basic Homemade Chicken Stock (page 98)

¾ cup fresh-squeezed orange juice

24 to 30 corn tortillas

Pickled Red Onions (page 123)

Roasted Habanero Salsa (page 123)

COOKING TIPS: *I've made this dish by grinding my own annatto seeds from scratch, but it doesn't taste like the Mexico City version. Most cooks there use ready-made achiote paste sold in rectangular bars at the markets. That's what I prefer, although the bars contain preservatives and technically aren't as pure as plain old achiote. You can find the bars online under the brands El Yucateco or Marin.*

Sour oranges, sold at Caribbean and Mexican supermarkets, taste less sour if they're too old. If they have brown spots inside, they're past their prime, in which case you can use this Sour Orange Substitute, below, whose ratios I found in David Sterling's excellent Yucatán cookbook. Don't leave out the banana leaves, which add a depth of flavor to the meat. You can find them at Caribbean or Mexican supermarkets, in the fresh or frozen foods aisle.

SOUR ORANGE SUBSTITUTE

This makes a decent approximation of a sour orange's tart-and-bitter taste. Use it only if you can't find fresh sour oranges.

½ cup fresh lime juice
¼ cup fresh-squeezed orange juice
¼ cup fresh-squeezed grapefruit juice

Mix the juices together in a large measuring cup or bowl. Refrigerate until ready to use.

PICKLED RED ONIONS

These tangy, sour onions add color and a burst of flavor to this citrusy slow-cooked pork. I also like them in salads, vegetable tacos or in quesadillas.

1 large red onion, sliced thinly
½ cup plus 1 generous tablespoon lime juice
⅔ cup fresh-squeezed orange juice
1 heaping teaspoon salt

Mix the onion, lime juice, orange juice and salt in a bowl. Refrigerate overnight or longer before serving. These will keep for a few months in an airtight container in the refrigerator.

ROASTED HABANERO SALSA

This fiery salsa was made for the tart, citrusy cochinita pibil, *but it's also excellent on eggs, beans or anywhere else you want a lot of heat. The salsa will keep for up to five days in an airtight container in the refrigerator.*

1   Heat a *comal* or nonstick skillet to medium or medium-high heat and, when hot, add the chiles and tomatillos in an even layer. Place the garlic near the edge of the *comal* so they don't burn. Cook, turning occasionally, until soft and blackened in spots.

2   Peel the garlic cloves and coarsely chop both the garlic and chiles. Add to a blender jar with the roasted tomatillos. Blend on high, adding a little water if necessary to help the blender blades turn. (Or adding more water if you want a thinner salsa.) Pour the salsa into a bowl and stir in salt to taste. Serve at room temperature.

5 habanero chiles
8 ounces tomatillos
2 cloves garlic, unpeeled
salt

MOLE VERDE CON POLLO
GREEN MOLE WITH CHICKEN

At local fondas, green mole is the second-most popular after mole poblano, served slathered over a chicken leg with a stack of warm corn tortillas. The ingredients depend on the cook—and the cook's hometown—but my favorite versions are bright, herbal and lightly tangy, and not too soupy. Green mole is quicker than other moles, since the fresh items go into the blender raw. You can also tweak the ingredients, substituting other greens for radish leaves, for instance, or fewer tomatillos if you want less tang. Vegetarians can serve this with slices of cooked squash, green beans, and fava beans.

1 (3½-pound) chicken, cut into 7 pieces

1 small wedge plus ½ medium onion

3 cloves garlic, peeled

3 poblano chiles

1 cup pumpkin seeds

2 tablespoons sesame seeds

1 teaspoon cumin seeds

1 pound and 12 ounces tomatillos, husked, rinsed, and coarsely chopped

3 large serrano chiles

1 small bunch radish leaves

4 romaine lettuce leaves

6 stems cilantro

2 sprigs epazote (about 10 leaves)

2 tablespoons lard or canola oil

2½ teaspoons salt, or more to taste

12 to 15 corn tortillas

1   Place the chicken in a large deep pot and cover with cold water. Add the small onion wedge and 1 garlic clove and bring to a boil. Cover, lower the heat, and simmer for 20 minutes. Remove the chicken, strain out 5 cups of the stock and set both aside.

2   Roast the chiles over a gas flame until blackened in spots, and then wrap in a dishcloth to sweat for 20 minutes, until the skins soften. Peel off the skin with the pads of your fingers, then remove and discard the seeds, stems and veins (see page 37 for instructions). Chop the chiles coarsely and set aside.

3   While the chiles sweat, toast the pumpkin seeds on low heat in a small frying pan, stirring often, until they turn slightly golden and start to pop. Transfer immediately to a bowl so they don't burn. Add the cumin seeds to the pan and toast until aromatic, then transfer to a separate bowl and set aside. Turn off the heat and pour the sesame seeds into the same pan, swirling them around the pan slowly, until they turn a light golden color. Transfer to another small bowl.

4   Grind the pumpkin seeds in a coffee or spice grinder until light and powdery. Scrape into a small bowl, and then do the same with the sesame seeds. (Grinding the seeds separately helps ensure the smoothest texture possible—you can skip this step if you have a high-powered blender such as a Vitamix.)

5   In a blender jar, working in batches, blend the vegetables—tomatillos, serranos, remaining 2 garlic cloves, poblanos, radish leaves, romaine leaves, cilantro, and epazote—with 1 cup of the reserved stock until smooth.

6   Add the ground pumpkin and sesame seeds along with the whole cumin seeds, and blend on high until very smooth.

7   Heat the lard in a large deep heavy-bottomed pot over medium heat. Add the contents of the blender jar in one quick pour. Add a little stock to the blender jar, swish the liquid around gently and pour the remnants into the pot as well. Bring to a boil, stirring constantly, until it thickens slightly, 10 minutes.

8   Stir in an additional 2 cups of the stock and season with the salt. Cook on very low heat for about 45 minutes, simmering gently and stirring often with a wooden spoon, taking care to ensure the *mole* doesn't stick or burn. Add the remaining stock gradually, once the *mole* thickens and the liquid starts to evaporate—the ideal texture should be slightly thicker than gravy. Add the chicken to the pot and cook until pools of fat form on the surface, about 5 minutes.

9   To serve, warm the tortillas and place in a cloth or basket. Place one breast, or a leg and a thigh, onto a dinner plate. Ladle lots of sauce on top. Pass the tortillas at the table.

COOKING TIP: *One of the mysteries of this* mole *is that sometimes the pumpkin seeds separate from the sauce, creating a half-chunky, half-watery mixture. Contrary to some advice I recently found in an older Mexican cookbook (translating from the Spanish): "According to tradition, you must stir in only one direction with a wooden spoon, and not keep entering and removing the spoon, or else the sauce will separate"—I've found it's important to keep the heat low and stir very often. If the pumpkin seeds do separate from the rest of the sauce, pour the sauce into a blender, give it a whirl, and then return to the pot.*

You may have some sauce left over, which you can use to feed a few more people (buy a couple extra chicken legs and thighs), or for simple enmoladas, *tortillas dredged in warm* mole, *folded on a plate, topped with more* mole.

CHAPTER 4

IN THE COUNTRY

I started a street food tourism company in Mexico City in 2010, and when I first started giving the tours, I was surprised to find out how many of the street and market vendors lived outside the city limits. Their commutes were brutal: at least ninety minutes from the State of Mexico, a neighboring state that wrapped around the capital like a cloche hat, and easily two hours one way from Milpa Alta, an area technically within Mexico City, but tucked at its southernmost edge. Or they lived in Xochimilco, about 45 minutes away depending on traffic, where some farmers grow produce and supply a few of the upscale restaurants I like in Mexico City.

I made friends with a nice young guy who sold dried chiles at the Medellín Market in Roma, and one day he invited me to his house in San Pedro Atocpan, a quiet town with cobblestone streets in Milpa Alta. (The town is best known for its large number of families who make *mole* paste and sell it at the *tianguis*.) To get there, my husband and I took the subway to Tasqueña and then switched to a *pesero*, one of the small, rumbly buses that penetrate the deeper nooks of the capital. After about an hour of cruising wide avenues and then smaller back streets, we trudged up a four-lane road that wound up a steep hill, past fields of cactus and larger hills blanketed in grass and brush. The sky stared a shade of blue rarely seen in the city center.

We were still in Mexico City, but technically closer to the Mexican state of Morelos when we walked into his family's large patio, planted with fruit trees. The air smelled like spices and dried chiles, and butter and yeast—his family also baked bread to sell in the neighborhood.

JUST FOR A TASTE

Over the next few years, I'd make several more trips to San Pedro and a few to the neighboring city of Milpa Alta, to eat and shop at the markets and visit. I bought sweet, canary-yellow tomatillos grown in nearby Morelos, and tried *atole de novia*, a warm beverage made from ground corn, chocolate and ground hazelnuts. At the Milpa Alta *tianguis*, I walked down the sidewalk open-mouthed, dumbstruck at how gorgeous everything was: squash flowers as big as my hand; blackened, charred tamales with whole fish inside; freshly killed rabbits with their fur still on. Piles of fresh mushrooms, grown nearby, lay next to fresh water-colored corn with purplish-red splotches, a shade I'd never seen before. We ate mushroom tamales drenched in green sauce, and caramel-colored, crunchy homemade *chicharrón*.

I don't want to romanticize the city's rural areas, many of which tend to be poor. Life there—and everywhere in the city—is not easy. But it's interesting to think that even in one of the most urban places in the world, the food can change, transform from something good and enjoyable to something electric and essential, capable of luring you onto a bumpy bus for two hours, just for a taste.

AGUA DE PIÑA CON PEREJIL
PINEAPPLE-PARSLEY COOLER

Every market in Mexico City, both in the city and the outskirts, sells aguas frescas, a drink of puréed fruit, sugar and water. Pairing parsley with pineapple is popular—the bitter, grassy stalks balance out the sweetness, leaving you with a drink that actually tastes healthy. Pineapple can vary in acidity, so it's best to taste and decide for yourself whether you want sugar. This agua fresca is best served within one or two days.

1 Combine the pineapple, water, and parsley in a blender jar and blend until very smooth. Taste, and if you think it needs sweetener, add 1 tablespoon sugar and continue blending, tasting, and adding more if desired.

2 Pour into a pitcher and serve cold, either refrigerated or over ice. You can also strain it, if you don't like the little parsley pieces. (I do.)

2 cups roughly chopped, very ripe fresh pineapple
1 quart cold water
⅓ cup fresh flat-leaf parsley leaves
sugar to taste

AGUA DE LIMÓN
LIME AND BROWN SUGAR COOLER

Most lime aguas frescas in Mexico City taste like a tangier version of lemonade. My recipe is slightly different as it uses brown sugar instead of white, giving the beverage a warm, molasses-y undertone. A pinch of lime zest amps up the lime flavor. The only slightly strange thing is the color—brown sugar turns the drink brown instead of light green. The yield works well for large groups, or divide the recipe in half if there are only two of you.

Working in batches if necessary, place all ingredients in the blender and blend until very smooth. Serve chilled or at room temperature.

3 quarts cold water
½ teaspoon lime zest
½ cup fresh lime juice
¼ cup plus 2 tablespoons raw sugar

COOKING TIP: *Smaller key limes tend to be more flavorful than the larger Persian limes often sold in the United States. Use key limes if you can find them. For a slightly sweeter taste, try using piloncillo, an unrefined Mexican cane sugar sold in cone-shaped packages at most Mexican grocers (see page 61 to learn how to grate or chop it), or dark brown sugar.*

ATOLE DE PINOLE
PINOLE ATOLE

Atole is a thick, warm, sweetened beverage traditionally served with tamales, and in the urban part of Mexico City, vendors usually sell the same two or three varieties—often Champurrado *(page 55) and Atole de Arroz. Moving further south, however, that changes. In Xochimilco and Milpa Alta, vendors sell* atoles *with fresh seasonal fruit mixed in. And they also sell* atole de pinole *(pea-NO-lay), a mix of milk or water and a powder made from toasted, ground corn—usually red corn—and cinnamon and sugar. If you did not grow up drinking* atole, *it can be difficult to imagine pairing this hearty beverage with food. I think it works well as a snack on a cold day, or at a party served with lots of tamales.*

2 cups whole milk
½ cup *pinole* (see Tip)
2 tablespoons masa harina,
  or 1 teaspoon cornstarch
2 to 3 tablespoons sugar, or
  to taste

1   Pour 1 cup milk into a medium bowl and add the *pinole* a little at a time, whisking after each addition. Once the *pinole* has dissolved, set aside.

2   Sprinkle the masa harina or cornstarch over ¼ cup water and whisk well.

3   Heat the remaining 1 cup milk with 1¼ cups water over medium heat in a medium saucepan. When hot, stir in the masa or cornstarch mixture, whisking constantly so the masa doesn't seize and cause lumps. When fully dissolved, stir in the *pinole*, milk and sugar. Simmer, stirring constantly and scraping the bottom of the pan so the *atole* doesn't stick and burn, for about 15 minutes or until the beverage has thickened and no longer tastes powdery. If you're using cornstarch, which thickens more heavily than masa harina, you may need a bit more water to reach the desired consistency.

4   Serve warm, ladled into mugs or heatproof glasses.

COOKING TIP: *You can find* pinole *at some Mexican grocery stores in the U.S. or online. I like the Rancho Gordo brand. The amount of sugar can vary, so you may need more or less sweetener than what's called for in this recipe. Leftover* pinole *can be whisked into water or milk and sipped cold, as a traditional Mexican energy drink. It also makes a wonderful ingredient in ice cream.*

The use of cornstarch in atole *is authentic to Mexico City.* Atole *made with masa harina will produce a slightly grainier texture.*

SALSA MACHA
TOASTED ÁRBOL CHILE SALSA

On a recent trip to Mexico City, I saw this deep red, sediment-like salsa at the long row of tortillerías *inside the Xochimilco Market. I had tried* salsa macha *before—the name roughly translates to "extremely bold, hot salsa"—but never with so many nuts and seeds. My friends and I bought some, along with some tortillas and tlacoyos, and over the course of a few hours we wound through Xochimilco's canals and spooned the oily salsa on everything. Even on a plain tortilla, it was powerful: toasty, smoky, garlicky. The salsa is simple to make at home. The only trick is to keep the chiles from burning, or else the sauce will taste bitter. A warning: this stuff is hot.*

1   Heat the oil in a medium saucepan over medium heat. Add the garlic clove and cook until dark-golden brown and blistered, about 2 minutes. Transfer to a small bowl and set aside.

2   Add the chiles and cook briefly, about 10 seconds, stirring constantly with tongs until they release a spicy aroma. Be careful not to burn them. Transfer the chiles to a bowl using a slotted spoon and reserve the cooking oil.

3   Cut the chiles into pieces using kitchen shears or a sharp knife, and coarsely chop the garlic. Place both, with any chile seeds, into a blender jar. Blend into a dry, crumbly mixture. It should be fairly fine—if the mixture is quite coarse, scrape down the sides of the blender and blend again.

4   Transfer the chile-garlic mix to a bowl and pour at least ¼ cup of the reserved chile oil on top. (The amount of oil is really up to you, but it should definitely come up at least ½ inch over the chile mixture.) Stir in the sunflower seeds and peanuts, and add salt to taste. Stir again until thoroughly combined. Serve at room temperature.

5   Store the salsa in an airtight container in a cool place for up to a week.

½ cup canola oil

1 large clove garlic, peeled

25 dried árbol chiles, stems snipped if they're very long

1 tablespoon raw unsalted sunflower seeds, toasted

1 tablespoon raw unsalted peanuts, toasted

salt

HOW TO PEEL XOCONOSTLES

The xoconostles *must be mostly charred and soft before peeling. Cut them in half and scoop out the black- and magenta-colored seed sack in the center. Then gently peel off the tough outer skin and any rough patches at the top of the fruit. A small spoon may also help scoop out the flesh from the skin. The edible part of the fruit should be a moist, pale pink.*

SALSA DE XOCONOSTLE
SOUR CACTUS FRUIT SALSA

Xoconostles are sour cactus fruits native to Central Mexico. They look like small prickly pears—reddish-green or pink when ripe—but the taste is more mouth-puckering than your average tuna. (The name of the fruit is pronounced "show-coh-NO-stlay"; it's a Nahuatl word.) When roasted, they smell like no other fruit I know of: a mix of sweet apricot and peach, with a hint of earth and smoke and char. In Mexico City, xoconostles are most commonly used in salsas or as a condiment in Mole de Olla (page 108); they're also common in the State of Mexico, Hildago, and Tlaxcala. Due to its sourness, this salsa works best when you want more acidity and punch (more than say, a regular green salsa). I like it with Barbacoa (page 154) or salty tortilla chips.

1 Warm a *comal* or nonstick skillet over medium heat. When hot, add the xoconostles and tomatillos, along with the garlic clove near the edge of the pan, away from direct heat. Cook, turning occasionally with tongs, until the tomatillos and garlic are blackened in spots and soft, about 12 minutes, then set aside. Raise the heat and keep cooking the xoconostles until very soft and black nearly all over, about 30 minutes—this will make them easier to peel later. Peel the garlic clove when cool enough to handle.

2 Heat the oil in a small frying pan over medium or medium-low heat. (This shouldn't be too hot, or else the chiles will burn.) When preheated, add the chiles and fry, turning constantly with tongs, just until they begin to emit a spicy aroma, 10 to 15 seconds. Transfer to a bowl or plate.

3 Cut the xoconostles and remove the seeds and skin (see opposite.) Place with the tomatillos, garlic clove and chiles in a blender jar and blend into a coarse, chunky mixture, adding up to 2 tablespoons water if desired to thin it out. Pour into a serving bowl and stir in the salt. Serve at room temperature.

COOKING TIP: *You can find xoconostles in select Mexican supermarkets and bodegas in the produce section—in New York they're generally not near the cactus fruits, but mixed among the herbs.*

3 xoconostles (sour cactus fruits)
6 small tomatillos, husked and rinsed
1 medium garlic clove, unpeeled
2 teaspoons canola oil
4 dried árbol chiles, stems removed
½ teaspoon plus a pinch of salt

CHICHARRÓN CASERA
HOMEMADE CHICHARRÓN

Large jagged sheets of chicharrón, or pork crackling, can be found at any Mexico City market. It's most often eaten as a snack—as a crunchy vehicle for guacamole and salsas—or in a guisado, when it's drenched in salsa and cooked until soggy, then spooned into a tortilla. Most vendors sell two varieties: light and puffy with no fat or meat clinging to the skin, and a meaty, fatty version. Only in the outskirts of the city have I seen homemade chicharrón and it turns out it's not too difficult to make. Homemade chicharrón is wonderful with pico de gallo, any salsa, guacamole, or cooked in green sauce (like the Enchiladas Verdes sauce, page 50) and served in a taco when soft. I've kept the pieces large on purpose here, as it's customary in Mexico to break off a piece with your hands, then dip it in a salsa or guacamole.

1½ to 2 pounds pork skin
2 cups canola oil
salt
salsa of choice or guacamole,
    optional

1   Preheat the oven to 250°F.

2   Cut the skin into large, wide pieces, about 6 inches long by 4 inches wide.

3   Place the skin on a rack set over a baking sheet and bake for 1 hour. Lower the heat to 200°F and bake for 2 to 3 more hours, until the skin is a dark caramel brown and the top is no longer moist or sticky. (The bottom may still be slightly moist with fat.) Wash the rack and baking sheet, return the rack to the pan, and set them next to the stove.

4   Heat the oil in a large Dutch oven over high heat. When very hot (at least 320°F), add a piece of pork skin. After about 30 seconds, it should bubble and puff up into a *chicharrón*. Flip if necessary to make sure both sides are cooked. Once puffy and golden brown, transfer to your prepared baking sheet and season with salt. Repeat with the remaining pieces of pork skin.

5   Serve as soon as the pieces have cooled, with salsa or guacamole if desired. Or store the pieces in an airtight container for snacking later. They will keep for up to 5 days.

COOKING TIP: *You'll need to find a butcher who sells pork skin and, if she doesn't slice off the fat for you, you'll need a very sharp knife and a lot of patience, unless you're particularly skilled at butchery. (I recommend buying the skin with the fat already scraped off, unless you prefer your chicharrón with a thin layer of fat or meat.)*

Deep-frying the chicharrón in lard, as cooks do in Mexico, boosts the pork flavor, but it's pungent and can be messy. For something slightly less porcine, try canola oil or another neutral oil suitable for frying.

SOPES DE MAÍZ AZUL
BLUE CORN SOPES

One summer day, I visited the farm of Abel Rodriguez and his wife, Emma Villanueva Buendía, who grow corn, beans and other crops in Tepetlixpa, a town about an hour and twenty minutes from Mexico City. Señora Villanueva made an almuerzo, *or mid-morning meal, of blue corn sopes—small, toasted masa disks spread with a thin layer of cooked beans, green salsa and a dollop of what might've been the best Mexican crema I'd ever had. (Her neighbor makes it from scratch; for my version, see opposite.) The sopes were rustic and comforting, reminding me that even the simplest food in Mexico can taste as good as the most complex.*

1 pound fresh blue corn tortilla masa or
    2 cups masa harina
1½ cups warm water, if using masa harina
1 batch Quick Refried Beans (page 45)
salsa of choice, such as Raw Tomatillo Salsa
    (page 26)
Homemade Crema (see opposite)
crumbled queso fresco, goat cheese, or any
    other salty, tangy cheese

1   If using fresh masa, place in a deep bowl and knead, adding a few drops of water, until airy and soft. To test if it's ready, break off a knob, roll into a ball and flatten. If the ball cracks at the edges, you need more water.

2   Alternatively, if using masa harina, place the dry flour in a deep bowl and pour about half the water on top. Mix in with a rubber spatula or wooden spoon, and then add the remaining water a little at a time, kneading the masa with your fingers. Test to see if it's adequately hydrated the same way as above. Once the dough is sufficiently moist, cover it with a damp dish towel so it doesn't dry out.

3   Heat a *comal* or nonstick skillet to medium-low heat. Place a clean cutting board near the stove.

4   Line both plates of a tortilla press with plastic sheets. Break off a piece of masa the size of a golf ball and roll it into a smooth ball. Place on one side of the press, then close and push down on the lever. Don't press them too thin—the ideal shape should be slightly thicker than your average tortilla.

5   Open the press and peel off the top plastic sheet. Gently pick up and flip the tortilla over onto your palm, positioning it so half hangs off the side. (This is tricky, but you'll get it with practice.) Gently peel off the remaining plastic sheet. (If the dough breaks or sticks to the sheet, it's too wet—you can add a bit of masa harina to dry it out, but if you're using fresh masa, be aware the taste will be affected.)

6   Making a sweeping motion with your hand, gently place the tortilla onto the hot *comal*. Cook for about 30 seconds, or until the tortilla darkens slightly and looks less moist, then flip. Cook for another 20 seconds then transfer to the cutting board. (The tortilla should still be half-raw at this point.) Let the tortilla cool for 1 minute, then dig into the edges and pinch the raw masa slightly upward, forming a raised border around the perimeter.

7 Place the *sope* back on the *comal* and continue cooking it for 4 to 5 minutes, until the outer skin is crisp and the *sope* no longer feels soft or mushy. These may be cooked ahead of time, cooled and refrigerated in a sealed container for 1 or 2 days, or longer if frozen.

8 Warm the refried beans or other toppings, as necessary. Spoon a thin layer of beans onto the *sope* and top with a drizzle of salsa. Finish with a spoonful of crema and a sprinkling of cheese. Serve immediately.

9 To reheat *sopes* that have been frozen, thaw first and sprinkle with a little water if they look dry. Then reheat on the *comal*.

COOKING TIPS: *My local* tortillería *in New York sells blue corn masa once a week, but if you can't find it where you live, feel free to use fresh yellow tortilla masa or masa harina. You can also top the* sopes *with whatever you want—I use beans, salsa and crema to mimic my original experience, but shredded, poached chicken, or fried potatoes and chorizo would work, too. Once cooked and filled, the* sopes *should be eaten immediately.*

HOW TO SHAPE SOPES

A sope *is like a thicker version of a tortilla, with raised edges. In Mexico, women pinch the edges directly on the* comal. *Unless you have extremely callused fingers and you're an expert at working with masa, you'll want to remove the half-raw tortilla from the stove first and pinch the edges on a separate workspace. It may take you a few tries to get the technique down. Don't give up if the first one doesn't come out perfectly.*

CREMA CASERA
HOMEMADE CREMA

The Mexican crema sold in U.S. supermarkets varies widely in quality. Some brands are very thick, like sour cream; others are thin and soupy. Still others don't taste much like dairy at all. I think it's easiest just to make your own. My favorite Mexican cremas have a lactic tang, so I've used yogurt to try and mimic that. The result is a bit tangier than using buttermilk, which is often what's called for when making crème fraîche. You can use this for any recipe that calls for crema. You'll need a glass jar with a lid; the crema lasts for about five days in the fridge.

1 Two days before you'd like to eat the crema, warm the cream in a small saucepan over medium-low heat. You should only heat to take the chill off; be careful not to overheat. Stir in the yogurt and turn off the heat.

2 Pour into a small, clean jar and let cool. Place the lid loosely on top, without tightening, and let sit for 24 hours in a warm place.

3 Place the crema in the fridge for at least 6 hours to thicken. Stir and add salt to taste (I like just a pinch) before serving.

1 cup heavy cream
1 tablespoon plain yogurt
   (not Greek)
salt

SOPA MILPA
SQUASH FLOWER AND VEGETABLE SOUP

This delicate soup is served during the rainy season in Milpa Alta. That's when squash is most tender, and the squash flowers bloom to an exaggerated, lush size. This recipe comes from my friend Erick Valle, whose family lives in nearby San Pedro Atocpan. The broth is light on purpose, as an intense or rich chicken flavor would overwhelm the vegetables. For vegetarians, a flavorful vegetable broth would work equally well. You can serve this soup to accompany something else, but I think it works fine as a light meal, with warm tortillas on the side.

1   Place the chicken in a large saucepan. Cover with 2 quarts cold water, add the spearmint, garlic and onion and season with salt. Bring to a boil, then lower the flame, cover and simmer for 25 minutes. Strain the chicken broth and discard the bones, meat and aromatics. Set aside.

2   In a large pot, heat the oil over medium-high heat. Add the squash, mushrooms, and corn and fry, stirring occasionally, until slightly softened, 3 to 4 minutes. Pour in the chicken broth, add the epazote and season with salt. Bring the soup to a boil, then cover, reduce the heat to low, and simmer for 5 minutes.

3   Add the squash blossoms, replace the lid, and simmer for 20 minutes or until the flavors meld. Taste and adjust the seasonings.

4   To serve, heat the corn tortillas on a *comal* or nonstick skillet until soft and pliable and place in a basket or cloth to keep warm. Ladle the soup into bowls and pass the corn tortillas at the table.

1 pound chicken parts, such as a
   chicken back and two wings
1 sprig spearmint
2 large cloves garlic
¼ medium onion
salt
2 tablespoons canola oil
1 pound round, tender young
   Mexican squash, cubed
½ pound white button or crimini
   mushrooms, thinly sliced
1½ cups corn kernels
1 sprig fresh epazote
2 large bunches of squash
   blossoms (about 10 ounces),
   torn into strips
12 to 16 corn tortillas

COOKING TIPS: *Most U.S. farmers' markets sell squash flowers toward the middle to end of summer, or you can find them in some specialty markets. The way they're sold and the size of the flowers can vary. The weight referenced here is for fairly large flowers with the stems on. In any case, count on needing at least two dozen.*

Most cooks in Mexico City tear their squash flowers by hand, instead of chopping them with a knife. I like the uneven texture that comes with tearing. To do so, break off the stem, and press on the base to gently open the flower into two pieces. Tear the petals into long strips, keeping the base intact if possible. Some people discard the stamen (the center part of the flower), but I like it. You definitely want to keep the green base of the flower in the soup—it adds a nice, firm texture.

MEXTLAPIQUES
GRILLED FISH TAMALES

The word mextlapique *refers to a type of tamal made with freshwater fish, stuffed into a corn husk and grilled on a* comal. *Historians trace them to before the Spaniards' arrival in 1521, and they're still made this same way in some parts of Mexico City—you can spot the vendors by their piles of blackened corn husks. The corn husk, in this case, acts as a sort of parchment, steaming the fish and vegetables. I like finishing these with a touch of olive oil and lime juice, and Creamy Jalapeño Salsa.*

12 to 15 large dried corn husks, 1 torn into strips

1½ to 2 pounds firm white fish fillets, such as cod or haddock, cut into 4 pieces

salt and freshly ground black pepper

1 cup fresh diced cactus (from 2 large paddles, rinsed and de-spined, see page 146)

¼ medium onion, cut into slivers

½ cup fresh diced tomato

1 jalapeño or serrano chile, cut into thin rounds

5 stems fresh epazote leaves, coarsely chopped

olive oil, for serving

3 to 4 limes, cut into wedges

1 batch Creamy Jalapeño Salsa (page 96), or salsa of choice

1   Place the corn husks in a large pot of hot water and let them soften for 45 minutes.

2   Season the fish with salt and pepper. Grab a corn husk and shake it dry. Nestle a fish fillet inside and top with a quarter of the cactus, onion slivers, diced tomato, and chile. Add 1 tablespoon of the chopped epazote leaves and sprinkle on a little more salt.

3   Close the husk by bringing the edges together and folding down the narrower end. If there are any holes in the husk, wrap in another corn husk. Tie a few strips of corn husk around the width of the *tamal* to keep it closed. Repeat three times to make the rest of the tamales.

4   Heat a *comal* or griddle to medium heat. Add the tamales directly to the *comal* and cook for 5 to 7 minutes on each side, or until the fish and vegetables are tender. The husks will burn and blacken, but that's part of the flavor and presentation.

5   To serve, place on individual plates and let the guests unwrap. Pass the olive oil, lime wedges, and salsa at the table. The tamales should be eaten out of the husk.

COOKING TIP: *Depending on the size of your corn husks, you may need to cut the fish into smaller pieces, in order for them to fit comfortably inside.*

TAMALES DE HONGOS
MUSHROOM AND GREEN SALSA TAMALES

July is rainy season in Milpa Alta and mushrooms are everywhere in the market. Local farmers sell them in bunches on small tarps: fat morels, smooth golden yemitas, fringey escobetilla (named as such because it looks like you could sweep the floor with it), and the long, thin mushroomy fingers of the clavito. On my first visit, I bought a mushroom tamal at a market stand with bits of clavito and dripping green salsa. It was a revelation: meaty and spicy and satisfying. These are particularly fantastic for breakfast, with a cup of Café de Olla (page 61). Any extra sauce can be served with the tamales, or stored and used for tacos, quesadillas, eggs, or anything else.

at least 36 dried corn husks

1 pound tomatillos, husked and rinsed

1 medium garlic clove, peeled

2 serrano chiles

¼ medium white onion

¼ cup Basic Homemade Chicken Stock (page 98) or water

2 teaspoons lard or canola oil

¼ teaspoon ground cumin

¾ teaspoon salt, or more to taste

10 ounces brown beech mushrooms, roots trimmed and mushrooms separated into individual stems, or crimini mushrooms cut into quarters

For the masa:

4 cups masa harina, or 3 pounds fresh masa for tamales

2 teaspoons baking powder

1½ teaspoons salt

3 cups room-temperature Basic Homemade Chicken Stock (page 98) for masa harina, 1¼ cups for fresh masa

1⅓ cups lard for masa harina, or 1½ cups if using fresh masa

1 Place the corn husks in a large pot of hot water to soften for 45 minutes.

2 Place the tomatillos, garlic, chiles, and onion in a large saucepan. Cover with cold water and bring to a boil, then lower the heat and simmer on medium until the tomatillos turn pea green and soften, about 12 minutes.

3 Stem the chiles and chop roughly with the garlic. Add to a blender jar with the tomatillos, onion, and stock. Blend until smooth.

4 Warm the lard or oil in a large skillet over medium heat. When melted, add the sauce in one quick pour. (Careful, it might splatter.) Stir in the cumin and salt and cook until the flavors meld, about 5 minutes. Transfer to a bowl and let cool.

5 Prepare the masa. If using masa harina, whisk together with the baking powder and salt in a large bowl. Working first with a spatula, and then with your hands, gradually add 3 cups stock, stirring and then kneading lightly until all liquid has been absorbed. Set aside for 10 minutes to allow the liquid to fully soak into the flour. If using fresh masa, moisten with about 1 cup stock, adding a little at a time. Knead well until soft, slightly sticky and pliable. (Depending on how dry the masa is, you may need an extra ¼ cup stock, or you may need a little less.)

6 Meanwhile, in a standing mixer equipped with the paddle attachment, whip the lard on medium speed until it's smooth and glossy, about 5 minutes. Increase the speed to high and integrate small, golf ball-size bits of masa into the lard a little at a time, mixing well after each addition, until a cohesive, very sticky dough forms. It should look similar to a thick muffin batter. Add more liquid if the dough looks too dry and dense.

7 If using fresh masa, now sprinkle the baking powder and salt onto the dough. Mix well for several more minutes, and taste to see if the masa needs more salt. If so, add and keep mixing until well combined. Dough made with masa harina can be stored in the refrigerator, tightly covered, for up to 24 hours or until ready to use. (You may need to add more stock when you're ready to use it—masa harina sucks up liquid quickly.) Dough made with fresh masa must be used the very same day or it will turn sour.

8   To form the tamales, lift some of the husks out of the pot and dry them lightly with a kitchen towel. Place a husk vertically in your hand. Add ¼ cup of masa and spread it, using the underside of a spoon, into a longish rectangle. Don't spread all the way to the edges, because the masa will expand in the pot, and you also need room to fold the husk over. Place 3 to 4 pieces of mushroom on top and cover with 1 tablespoon of the sauce.

9   Clutch both of the long edges of the husk and fold them over each other, so that the masa covers the filling. The *tamal* should fold cleanly and securely, and the filling should not drip out. If it does, you've added too much. (You can open the husk and remove some, if so.)

10   Once closed, fold down the narrower end of the corn husk and press along the fold to seal. (With the thicker, more manicured corn husks, you may need to tie these closed with an extra strip of husk.) Look over the tamal carefully to make sure there aren't any holes where masa could seep out during cooking. If there are holes, wrap the tamal in another leaf. The finished tamal should look elongated, like a slightly flattened sausage. Set aside on a baking sheet and repeat to make about 24 tamales. (See page 143 for photos.)

11   Add water to the steamer pot and place a coin in the bottom; the coin will rattle when the water starts to boil. Very carefully, place the tamales in a loose vertical position in the steamer pot, with the folded sides touching the pot floor. Cover with more husks, then a layer of plastic wrap, then the lid. If the pot has a side opening for the purpose of adding water, cover it with aluminum foil.

12   Steam for 50 to 60 minutes on high heat. (At higher altitudes, this may take longer.) Listen to the pot occasionally to make sure the coin keeps rattling; if not, add more water, taking extreme care not to dampen the tamales. To check for doneness, remove one *tamal* from the pot and open the husk. If it peels back cleanly, without sticking, the *tamal* is done.

13   Let cool for at least 15 minutes before serving. Serve in the husk, with plenty of salsa.

COOKING TIPS: *This recipe uses brown beech mushrooms, which are a smaller version of the clavito that's available in the United States, particularly at Asian supermarkets. If you can't find them, use crimini or another flavorful mushroom (not white button). Boxed chicken stocks can overwhelm the delicate mushroom flavor, so avoid those here if possible. Like any tamal recipe, this works much faster if you've got a friend to help you stuff them. You'll need a large steamer pot but if you don't have one, see the Cooking Tip on page 37.*

AYOCOTES CON NOPALES
RUNNER BEANS WITH CACTUS

Large, starchy ayocote beans are like the butter bean of Mexico. They've got a bit of a stronger flavor, but the creamy innards are just as seductive. I have eaten ayocotes—known in English as runner beans—many times, but I particularly love this combination, prepared at the home of Emma Villanueva Buendía, who, along with her husband Abel, farms corn in Tepetlixpa, in the State of Mexico just outside Mexico City. She seasons the beans only with a bit of onion and a Mexican bay leaf, which infuses its flavor into the broth. The cactus, meanwhile, thickens the bean broth with its viscous sap. It's delicious with a helping of Mexican rice on the side.

4 cactus paddles (about
    14 ounces)
1 pound dried purple *ayocote*
    (runner) beans (see Tip),
    rinsed and soaked overnight
salt
2 teaspoons lard or canola oil
¼ medium onion, chopped
1 dried Mexican bay leaf
12 to 16 corn tortillas
1 batch Mexican-style Red Rice
    (page 97)

COOKING TIP: *You should be able to find runner beans at most Mexican grocery stores, online at Rancho Gordo or at specialty grocers. They're usually black, purple or white.*

1   De-spine and rinse the cactus paddles (see below for photos), then cut them into 1½-inch by ¼-inch pieces. Set aside.

2   Drain the beans, place in a large pot and cover with 3 to 4 inches fresh cold water. Bring to a boil, then lower the heat to medium or medium-low, ensuring that the beans bubble gently. Cook until creamy and tender, about 2 hours, seasoning with salt in the last 5 to 10 minutes of cooking. Pour the beans and cooking broth into a large bowl and wipe out the pot.

3   Heat the lard or oil in the same pot over medium-high heat. Add the onion and cook until blistered and dark-golden brown. Pour in the beans, add the bay leaf, and bring to a boil. Stir in the cactus and a light sprinkling of salt, if desired. Cook until the cactus is tender, 15 to 20 minutes. Taste and add more salt if necessary.

4   Warm the tortillas on a *comal* or nonstick skillet until soft and pliable, and place in a cloth or basket. Serve the soup in shallow bowls, ladling in beans, a good amount of broth and cactus into each bowl, along with a generous helping of Mexican rice on the side. Pass the warm tortillas at the table.

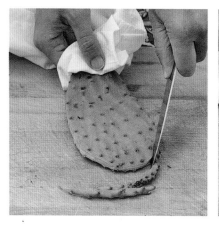  

NOPALES Y VERDURAS EN ESCABECHE
PICKLED CACTUS AND VEGETABLES

Milpa Alta, the southernmost region in Mexico City, is a massive cactus-growing region. One of my favorite ways to eat cactus there is en escabeche, or lightly pickled in vinegar. The chopped paddles are tossed with other veggies, such as fava beans, carrots, or cauliflower. The mixture is so good—a balance of sweet, spicy, and tangy, without being overly briny—that you can eat piece after piece, assuming you can handle the heat. Traditionally nopales en escabeche is served as a topping for your taco, or a nibble to complement whatever you're eating. I like it slightly warm, spooned into a corn tortilla and eaten as its own taco, perhaps with a soup or a little Mexican rice on the side. You can also serve this cold or at room temperature.

1   Remove the thorns from the cactus paddles (see opposite for photos), rinse, and cut into 3-inch by 1-inch pieces. Fill a medium saucepan two-thirds full with water. Add the onion, garlic, and salt and bring to a vigorous boil. Add the cactus and cook until just barely tender, about 2 minutes. Using a slotted spoon, transfer the cactus to a plate and discard the aromatics.

2   To make the *escabeche*, heat the oil in a medium, heavy-bottomed pot over medium-high heat. Add the onions and cook until translucent, 6 to 8 minutes, stirring occasionally. Add the garlic and jalapeños and cook until aromatic, about 1 minute. Stir in the fava beans, carrots, cactus, salt, allspice, thyme, marjoram and bay leaves, making sure the vegetables are evenly coated in oil. Turn the heat to medium-low, cover, and cook for about 8 minutes, until the flavors combine. Stir in the vinegar and olive oil. Taste and adjust the seasonings.

3   Serve either warm or cold. The mixture will keep refrigerated in an airtight container for up to 2 weeks.

COOKING TIPS: *For pickling cactus, it's traditional to use cane sugar vinegar (vinagre de caña), a slightly sweet vinegar sold at Asian markets in the U.S. If you can't find it, apple cider vinegar will work.*

The favas should not be peeled all the way, as is common in Central Mexico—locals love the beans' outer waxy skin, which adds flavor and texture. If the beans are young enough, they should not taste bitter. If you can't find favas, try adding cauliflower, green beans, or fresh peas.

I used red jalapeños because they're slightly hotter than the green variety, and they add a burst of color. If you can't find them or you want less heat, green jalapeños are fine.

4 to 5 cactus paddles (about 13 ounces)

1 thick slice onion

2 large cloves garlic, peeled

1 teaspoon salt

For the *escabeche*:

¼ cup canola oil

2 medium onions, sliced into thin rounds

4 medium cloves garlic, peeled

6 red jalapeños, stems removed, and cut lengthwise into ½-inch-thick wedges

2 pounds young, fresh fava beans, husked

2 to 3 large carrots, sliced medium-thick on the diagonal

1 tablespoon salt

6 allspice berries

3 stems fresh thyme

2 stems fresh marjoram

6 Mexican bay leaves

¼ cup plus 2 tablespoons cane vinegar or apple cider vinegar

¼ cup mild olive oil

CHORIZO VERDE
HOMEMADE GREEN CHORIZO

Green chorizo—colored green because it contains green chiles and vegetables—is typical to the city of Toluca in neighboring Mexico State. You can find it at Mexico City markets or at certain street stands specializing in chorizo. Typically it's crumbled and cooked, and served in a taco with a squirt of lime and a heavy spoonful of salsa.

I interviewed a half-dozen Toluca sausage makers to learn the secret behind the recipe, and all said they first create a mole-like sauce with herbs, spices and tomatillo, which they then add to the sausage. Tomatillo made my sausage too moist, so I've substituted spinach, which still gives the chorizo a nice light green color. Some cooks also add food coloring, which makes the meat look neon green—that could be fun for holidays or for kids. This makes quite a bit of sausage; leftovers can be frozen, or used in other non-Mexican dishes such as pasta, as breakfast patties or in sauces.

1 Roast the poblano over an open gas flame until blackened in spots, then wrap in a dish towel to sweat (see page 37 for instructions). Peel off the skin and make a slit to remove the seeds and veins. Chop coarsely and add to a blender jar with the serrano, garlic, onion, spinach, cilantro, cumin, peppercorns and oregano. Blend and taste, then add ¾ teaspoon salt, or to taste, and blend again until smooth. If the sauce doesn't break down right away, scrape down the insides of the blender jar and blend again. (Water can make the sausage soggy, so try not to use any unless you absolutely have to.)

2 Place the sauce in the refrigerator for at least 1 hour. At the same time, place the meat, fat, meat grinder (if using) and mixing bowl in the freezer for 1 hour. If using already ground meat, proceed to step 4.

3 Remove the items from the freezer, add the meat and fat to the grinder, and grind as per manufacturer's instructions.

4 Stir in 1¼ teaspoons salt, the peanuts, and the pecans. Using a standing mixer fitted with the paddle attachment, or by hand if desired, mix the cold sauce and apple cider vinegar into the ground meat until fully absorbed and slightly sticky. At this point the sausage can be refrigerated in an airtight container for up to 2 days, or longer if frozen.

5 Heat a large skillet to medium heat. Add the sausage in a more or less even layer—you may have to cook it in batches—and cook, stirring often, until the sausage is no longer pink and slightly crisp in spots, 7 to 10 minutes.

6 Serve in tortillas, passing lime wedges and salsa at the table.

COOKING TIP: *If you don't have a meat grinder, ask the butcher to grind a very fatty cut of pork shoulder, or, even better, to blend 2 pounds shoulder with 8 ounces pork fat. Casings aren't needed, since you're going to crumble the sausage. If you're a more skilled sausage maker, you could try casing the sausage, let it age for two to three days, then cook it.*

It's important that the sausage and sauce be very cold when you're mixing it, otherwise it may not bind together correctly.

1 small poblano chile
1 large serrano chile, roughly chopped
1 garlic clove, roughly chopped
⅛ medium onion, roughly chopped
1 cup packed spinach leaves
2 large stems fresh cilantro
¼ teaspoon cumin seeds
⅛ teaspoon peppercorns
¼ teaspoon dried Mexican oregano
salt
2 pounds pork shoulder, cut into large cubes
8 ounces pork fat, cut into large cubes (see Tip)
½ cup raw unsalted peanuts, toasted and roughly chopped
½ cup roughly chopped pecans
2 tablespoons apple cider vinegar
30 corn tortillas, warmed
7 limes, cut into wedges
salsa of choice

MIXIOTES DE VERDURAS
STEAMED PACKETS OF CHICKEN AND VEGETABLES

A mixiote *is usually a steamed packet of meat draped in a pungent, spicy chile sauce. It's steamed in the papery peel of the maguey leaf, also called* mixiote, *hence the name. Mixiotes are very common in the Central Mexican states of Hidalgo, Tlaxcala, Puebla, and in the State of Mexico, and you can find them throughout Mexico City, particularly at* fondas *or restaurants specializing in rustic food.*

It's not wholly common to find a mixiote *with so many vegetables, but I've found myself missing them every time I open a* mixiote *and find nothing but meat. This recipe, which calls for chorizo or chicken, riffs a little on the flavors and sauces found in* mixiotes *in Mexico City, and speaks more to my specific tastes. I like to serve these with corn tortillas on the side.*

8 guajillo chiles

2 morita chiles

1 ripe plum tomato

2 large cloves garlic, unpeeled

¼ medium onion

3 cups packed, chopped chard leaves

2 cups cauliflower florets

1 large Mexican squash, cut into quarters about ½-inch wide

1 cup fresh diced cactus (about 2 paddles, de-thorned and rinsed, see page 146)

1 cup fresh or frozen peas

salt and freshly ground black pepper

1½ pounds small boneless, skinless chicken thighs or chorizo sausages

2 teaspoons canola oil, plus more if necessary

¼ teaspoon ground Mexican cinnamon

2 cloves

1 teaspoon fresh thyme

4 limes, cut into wedges

12 to 16 corn tortillas, warmed

1   Cut out 6 large squares of parchment paper roughly 14 by 15 inches each. Set aside.

2   Toast the chiles briefly on a *comal* or nonstick skillet over medium to medium-low heat, just until they release a spicy aroma, 15 to 30 seconds. (Turn frequently so they don't burn.) Transfer to a workspace, then add the tomato, garlic, and onion to the *comal*. Cook, turning occasionally, until charred in spots, about 5 minutes. Set aside to cool.

3   Snip the stems off the chiles, then make a slit to discard the seeds and veins. Place the chiles in a bowl of warm water until the skins soften, 20 to 30 minutes. Reserve the soaking water.

4   Meanwhile, add the chard, cauliflower, squash, cactus, and peas to a bowl and toss with salt and pepper to taste.

5   Cut the chicken thighs into 4 pieces each and season liberally with salt. Heat a skillet over medium-high heat, and add the oil. Working in batches, cook the chicken just until golden brown, about 3 minutes per side. (No need to cook them through; they'll finish in the steaming process.) Alternatively, if using chorizo, slice open the sausages and discard the casings. Crumble into large pieces and fry over medium-high heat until dark golden-brown in spots. Set aside.

6   Place the softened chiles, 1 cup of the chile water, the tomato, garlic, onion, cinnamon, cloves, thyme, and ¼ teaspoon black pepper in a blender jar. Blend into a smooth yet still slightly thick sauce. Season with salt.

7   Add water to a steamer pot and bring to a boil over high heat.

8   Meanwhile, make a workspace with the parchment paper, veggies, chicken, and the sauce nearby. Place 1 piece of parchment paper on the workspace. Add 1 heaping cup of vegetables, 4 pieces of chicken or a small handful of chorizo, and ¼ heaping cup of sauce, being sure to cover the vegetables and meat.

9 Bring up the edges of the paper to form a little pouch and tie closed tightly with kitchen twine. Set aside and repeat until you have 6 pouches.

10 Carefully place the pouches in the steamer pot and cover tightly. Steam for 20 minutes, or until the peas are tender.

11 Serve immediately, placing a pouch on each plate for guests to unwrap. Pass the lime wedges and warm tortillas at the table.

COOKING TIP: *It's very hard to find* mixiote *leaves outside Mexico—and even within Mexico, they're increasingly over-harvested—so I use parchment paper, with good results. You'll also need kitchen twine and a steamer pot or basket insert.*

PESCADO AL MOJO DE AJO
GARLICKY PAN-FRIED FISH

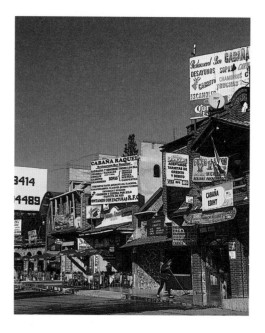

Driving west in Mexico City, past the city limits that end near the corporate, skyscraper-filled Santa Fe neighborhood, a pine forest unfolds. It's jarring: just a few minutes ago, there had been a mall, and now you're in a thatch of fog, whizzing past majestic green trees. This is the State of Mexico, home to thousands of Mexico City commuters, and also home to several gastronomic delicacies—among them different preparations of trout, raised in nearby farms. In places like La Marquesa, a row of colorful roadside food stands just beyond the outskirts of Mexico City, or in the nearby city of Malinalco, you can order trout with garlic sauce, chipotle sauce, grilled, or nearly any other way you want it, with a simple lettuce and tomato salad on the side.

In the U.S., it can be difficult to find this delicate freshwater fish year-round, depending on where you live. For this recipe, I've substituted cod, which has a firmer flesh but still stands up well under the mountain of garlic. Using whole fish instead of fillets would also work beautifully; that's how many fondas and restaurants do it in Mexico.

For garlic mojo sauce:

1 head garlic, or about 8 large cloves, roughly chopped
2 tablespoons fresh lime juice
2 tablespoons olive oil
½ teaspoon salt

1½ to 2 pounds firm white fish fillets such as cod, cut into 4 even pieces
salt and freshly ground black pepper
2 tablespoons canola oil, plus more if needed
6 large cloves garlic, thinly sliced
fresh parsley, chopped

1 First, prepare the sauce. Place the garlic and lime juice in a blender jar and blend to a chunky purée. Add the olive oil and blend to a smooth paste. Taste and season with the salt, and blend once more. Scrape the sauce into a bowl and set aside.

2 Season the fish fillets with salt and pepper.

3 Heat a large nonstick or cast-iron skillet over medium-high heat, and add the oil when hot. Add the garlic and cook until aromatic, lightly crisp, and brown, about 1 minute, then transfer to a small bowl. Keep the oil in the pan.

4 Fry the fish fillets in two batches, about 5 minutes per side, until a golden crust forms and fish is just cooked through. Cover lightly with aluminum foil to keep warm while you fry the second batch.

5 To serve, spoon a light layer of the garlic sauce on top of the fish, and top with the fried garlic and some parsley.

COOKING TIP: *This preparation—which calls for crispy garlic and a separate garlic sauce—does not exactly mirror the* mojo de ajo *presentations I've seen in Mexico, which feature crispy bits of garlic and little other seasoning. I've added a bit more oomph to reflect my taste. Be careful, though—the garlic sauce is intense, and a little goes a long way.*

Use a nonstick skillet or a well-seasoned cast-iron skillet to cook skinned fish fillets. They tend to stick in a regular stainless-steel frying pan.

CONEJO A LA BANDOLERA
BEER-BRAISED RABBIT

Tláhuac is perhaps the hardest borough to reach in Mexico City. Driving from the Centro can take around two hours with traffic, and the subway station that opened in 2013 closed a year later due to structural problems. Thankfully, there is an oasis for Tlahuaqueños, or at least people who can afford to dine there—a large restaurant called La Playa, located at the edge of a small lake where ducks swim. The owner, a slim middle-aged man named Juan Carlos Martinez, cracks jokes with the customers and occasionally offers a free shot of tequila. The place also serves a surprisingly large variety of more rustic foods: rabbit, grilled tamales, and edible insects such as maguey worms and ant larvae. This is one of the better rabbit dishes I've tried in Mexico City. The meat is fried, then braised slowly in beer until tender, giving the meat a slight yeastiness. The cook, Hortencia Zepahua, graciously explained the preparation for me.

1   Rinse the rabbit pieces and pat dry with paper towels. Season with salt, making sure to salt both sides.

2   In a large heavy skillet, melt the lard, olive oil, and butter over medium-high heat. Add the rabbit pieces in an even layer and cook undisturbed, 4 to 6 minutes, until a golden-brown crust forms. Be careful as the grease may pop and splatter. Turn and fry the other side until golden, another 4 to 5 minutes.

3   Add the bay leaf, fresh herbs, peppercorns, beer and ¼ cup water. Lower the flame to low, cover and cook for 20 minutes. Turn the rabbit pieces and cook, covered, for an additional 20 to 25 minutes, until tender when pierced with a fork.

4   Serve warm, spooning sauce over the meat, with Mexican rice on the side.

COOKING TIP: *To prepare the rabbit, you'll need a large skillet with deep sides and a lid. You should be able to find rabbit at a specialty butcher shop—ask the butcher to cut it into pieces.*

2 pounds rabbit, cut into pieces
salt
1 tablespoon lard
2 tablespoons olive oil
2 tablespoons unsalted butter
1 dried Mexican bay leaf
1 sprig fresh Mexican oregano, chopped
3 sprigs fresh marjoram, chopped
3 sprigs fresh thyme, chopped
2 peppercorns
¾ cup light beer, such as Victoria
1 batch Mexican-style Red Rice (page 107)

BARBACOA
SLOW-ROASTED MUTTON

In Mexico City, barbacoa is usually made from lamb or mutton, although occasionally you'll see it done with beef or goat. The dish—typically made from meat slow-roasted in a pit in the ground—is consumed with gusto on the weekends, where it's often sold in tacos or with a steaming bowl of consommé, made from the meat juices mixed with rice and garbanzo beans. Traditionally, the meat is freshly slaughtered and wrapped in maguey leaves while it bakes. Outside of Mexico, many of us don't have access to freshly slaughtered meat, a hole in the ground or maguey leaves. But it's still possible to recreate some of the same flavors at home, using a heavy Dutch oven pot with a lid, or a roasting pan covered tightly in aluminum foil.

I like using mutton—the gamier flavor reminds me a little more of the countryside in Mexico. The meat slow-roasts for four hours in the oven, and from there you make an easy consommé out of the resulting juices. All you need to complete the meal are lime wedges, salsa (traditionally Salsa Borracha, recipe opposite) and good corn tortillas. It makes for a stunning, comforting meal for large groups.

3 to 4 pounds mutton or lamb
    shanks (see Tip)
salt
6 or 7 avocado leaves (see Tip)
½ medium onion, cut into 2
    pieces, plus 1 cup diced onion
1 dried Mexican bay leaf
2 garlic cloves, peeled
2 thick sprigs fresh thyme
¼ cup dried chickpeas
½ cup long-grain white rice
¾ cup roughly chopped fresh
    cilantro
5 limes, cut into wedges
1 batch Salsa Borracha (see
    opposite), or salsa of choice
36 corn tortillas, warmed

COOKING TIPS: *Mutton is generally available at specialty or halal butcher shops in the U.S. If you can't find it, lamb is a fine (if more expensive) substitute. Avocado leaves should be available at Mexican markets, usually in the spice section.*

1   Adjust the oven rack to the middle or lower third of the oven and preheat to 275°F. Season the meat liberally with salt and set aside.

2   Heat a small skillet over medium-low heat and toast the avocado leaves until they smell aromatic. Set aside.

3   Place the mutton or lamb in a large Dutch oven (don't worry if the pieces overlap). Pour 3 cups water on top and add the onion wedges, bay leaf, garlic and thyme. Arrange the toasted avocado leaves on top of the meat. Cover tightly with heavy-duty foil and place the lid on top. Cook until the meat is tender and falling off the bone, 3½ to 4 hours.

4   Meanwhile, place the chickpeas in a medium bowl and cover with water. Let soak while the meat cooks, ideally for 4 hours, then drain.

5   Remove the meat carefully from the cooking liquid and transfer to a bowl. Ladle ½ cup of the cooking liquid over the meat and let cool slightly, then tear the meat into large pieces and cover with aluminum foil. Set the bones aside—do not discard.

6   Warm the remaining cooking liquid over medium heat. Remove the thyme stems and add the bones and 2 quarts water. Bring to a boil, then add the rice and soaked chickpeas. Return to a boil, then reduce the heat to medium-low. Simmer gently, uncovered, for about 1 hour, until the chickpeas are soft. (If the consommé has reduced too much, add a little more water.) Season with salt— the broth should be nice and salty.

7   Place the mutton on a platter and the cilantro, diced onion, lime wedges and salsa on the table, with the warm tortillas. Ladle consommé into small heatproof bowls to serve guests individually to start, and let guests make their own tacos with the mutton, garnishes and tortillas.

SALSA BORRACHA
"DRUNK" SALSA

This bitter, intense salsa traditionally calls for pulque, *the fermented, lightly alcoholic sap from the agave plant. Since pulque is next to impossible to find outside Mexico City (save for canned varieties, which I stay away from), I've substituted dark Mexican beer. You can make this lots of ways, but I like the textures and saltiness that come from using slightly aged cheese, pickled chiles, and raw onion. If you like softer flavors, add a spritz of fresh-squeezed orange juice.*

1   Toast the chiles briefly on the *comal* or in a nonstick skillet over medium-low heat. They should not burn—turn them almost constantly until they release a spicy aroma, 5 to 10 seconds. Remove, snip off the stems, and shake out and discard the seeds. Fill a bowl with warm water and let the chiles soak until the skins soften, about 20 minutes.

2   Meanwhile, toast the garlic on the *comal* until soft and squishy, 5 to 8 minutes.

3   Place the garlic, chiles, oil, and beer in a blender, and blend until smooth. Transfer to a bowl and stir in the pickled jalapeños and onion. (Taste and add the orange juice if you like.) Stir in the salt as desired and top with the cheese.

4   The salsa is best if eaten immediately.

5 pasilla chiles
2 garlic cloves, unpeeled
1½ teaspoons olive oil
½ cup plus 2 tablespoons dark Mexican beer, such as Negra Modelo
¼ cup coarsely chopped pickled jalapeños
chopped onion, to taste
3 tablespoons fresh-squeezed orange juice, optional
½ teaspoon salt, or more to taste
¼ cup crumbled queso añejo

PLÁTANO MACHO CON LECHE CONDENSADA
FRIED PLANTAIN WITH CONDENSED MILK AND JAM

I first spotted this dessert at a rustic outdoor restaurant in Texcoco, a small city northeast of the capital. A cook stood in front of a huge metal fryer set over an open flame, filled with thick slices of plantain. As a line of people watched, the cook removed a plantain slice from the bubbling oil, topped it with spoonfuls of condensed milk, and finished with a dollop of chunky fruit preserves. The mixture was simple but heavenly: fruity and rich, the fruit creamy-fleshed from its time in the fryer.

2 large, very ripe plantains
canola oil
1 (14-ounce can) sweetened
    condensed milk
generous ¼ cup strawberry or
    blackberry fruit preserve

1 Peel the plantains and cut them, from pole to pole, into three long pieces measuring ¼ to ½ inch thick.

2 Heat a large skillet to medium or medium-high heat. Pour enough canola oil to coat the bottom about ⅛-inch deep. Line a plate with paper towels.

3 When hot, add the plantain slices in batches—they should sizzle or else the oil isn't hot enough. Cook until dark-golden brown, 2 to 3 minutes per side. Drain on the prepared plate.

4 Place one warm plantain on a small serving plate and spoon a generous helping of condensed milk on top. Finish with a heaping tablespoon of fruit preserve.

COOKING TIP: *At home, I've tried substituting bananas instead of plantains, but the flavor isn't the same, and bananas turn rather flaccid when pan-fried. Make sure your plantains are as ripe as possible—the outer skin should be black. I like tart fruit preserves with this, such as blackberry or strawberry.*

CHAPTER 5

AT
HOME

Even though I grew up in a Mexican-American household in Southern California, we did not eat much Mexican food. My mom was usually too busy to cook so we ate TV dinners and hot dogs and frozen burritos, and sometimes one-pot stews with vegetables from our garden. Sometimes I wrapped our hot dogs in flour tortillas, because we didn't always have hot dog buns. Every now and then my mom bought jalapeños or canned, spicy peppers, but I stayed far away—I hated spicy food.

Once I started living on my own and cooking for myself, I realized that a homemade meal was a way to pamper myself, my friends, or my boyfriend at the end of a hectic day. I began experimenting, sampling foreign cuisines, buying wine for weeknight dinners. I bought a few Mexican cookbooks that I sometimes dug out for Cinco de Mayo.

When my husband and I moved to Mexico, I thought: Would they sell my organic cereal there? What about quinoa? By the time I moved back to the States four years later, my eating habits had changed. I didn't eat much quinoa anymore. I ate beans. My breakfast had morphed into roasted poblano pepper oatmeal, or at the very least scrambled eggs drizzled with salsa.

In New York, I craved the Mexican ingredients that had begun to taste like home to me: fresh corn tortillas (the ones made from real, nixtamalized corn), stewed beans, cactus, tomatillos, serranos, roasted poblanos, guava, dried chiles. Those cravings weaved into my pre-Mexico way of eating, which usually combined vegetables and legumes and little meat. Mexican flavors permeated other culinary interests, too: Indian and Middle Eastern foods, and those from the American South, where my husband is from.

At home in New York, I combine cultures as much as I want. I shop at Mexican and Indian grocery stores, Asian and farmers' markets (luckily all of these are within walking distance of my house). Most of the dishes that follow I make on a weeknight, when I'm eyeing the fridge like we all do, wondering what to cook.

PRICKLY PEAR AGUA FRESCA WITH LIME AND CHIA SEEDS

Prickly pear cactus fruit, known in Spanish as tuna, is especially abundant during Mexico City's rainy season, when you can often get two pounds for less than a dollar. The flesh is moist and mildly sweet, sort of like a more floral version of watermelon. Some people peel and eat the fruit raw, and many use it in an agua fresca. At home in New York, the Mexican bodegas near my house sell prickly pear fairly inexpensively, which means I can recreate the drink most times of the year. I like adding in chia seeds and a little lime juice. The amount of fruit you include can vary, since some tunas may be riper and muskier than others.

3 pounds green or red prickly pear fruit, peeled and cut into large chunks (see sidebar)
2 tablespoons sugar
2 tablespoons fresh lime juice
2 tablespoons chia seeds

1   Put the fruit, sugar, lime juice, and 1 quart water in a blender jar. Blend until smooth, taste for more sugar or lime juice and blend again. Strain into a pitcher using a fine-mesh strainer.

2   Stir the chia seeds into pitcher. Serve cold or over ice.

HOW TO PEEL PRICKLY PEAR FRUIT

Tunas have a very thick skin, which must be peeled to get to the moist, seed-dotted flesh inside. To peel, slice into the fruit from pole to pole with a paring knife. You'll want to slice deeply, almost ¼ inch into the fruit—don't just cut into the thin outer layer. If the tuna is ripe, you should be able to open the fruit up like a package, peeling off the thick skin like a wrapper. You will be left with a small, oval-shaped fruit, dotted with dark seeds.

SPICY CHIPOTLE BEAN DIP

I'm often looking for new ways to use leftover cooked beans in my fridge, and I threw together this dip one evening when friends were coming over to watch the basketball game. The mix of dried chipotle and chipotle en adobo means you get a lot of smoke in every bite, but you don't get too much acid or vinegar, which would compete with the creaminess of the beans. This would work well as a shmear for a wrap, burger or sandwich, too.

1   Prepare the tortilla chips, if you haven't already.

2   Heat a *comal* or nonstick skillet to medium-low heat and when hot, toast the chipotle meco chiles lightly, until they release a spicy aroma, 5 to 10 seconds per side. Place in a bowl of warm water and let soften, 15 to 20 minutes. Strain and reserve about ½ cup of the chile water. Set aside.

3   Heat the lard in a medium saucepan over medium-high heat. Add the garlic and onion and cook, stirring occasionally, until dark golden and blistered on all sides, about 3 minutes.

4   Add the beans and broth in one quick pour. Stir in the black pepper, cumin, and a pinch of salt. Bring to a boil, then lower the heat, cover, and simmer for 5 minutes to let the flavors meld. Let cool to room temperature.

5   Pour the cooled bean mixture, chipotle, soaked chiles, and the reserved chile water into a blender jar and blend until smooth. Taste for more salt or cumin if desired.

6   To serve, pour the bean dip into a bowl and serve with the chips.

Baked Tortilla Chips (recipe
  follows)
2 chipotle meco chiles, seeds
  and stems removed
2 teaspoons lard or canola oil
2 cloves garlic, peeled
¼ medium onion
2 cups cooked black beans,
  with about ¾ cup bean broth
⅛ teaspoon black pepper
½ teaspoon ground cumin
salt
1 large chipotle en adobo from
  a can, with seeds

COOKING TIP: *The dish is very spicy, because that's how I like things. Feel free to use less chipotle or remove the seeds to reduce the heat.*

BAKED TORTILLA CHIPS

These crunchy chips are my go-to snack at home, and baking them gives them a nutty flavor. It's also a great way to use any old tortillas lying around in the fridge. I usually don't add salt, but you can if you want more punch.

1   Preheat the oven to 425°F. Stack 6 tortillas into a pile and use a large sharp knife to carefully cut the whole stack into 8 even triangles. Spread in an even layer on a baking sheet. (If you have two baking sheets, cut the remaining six tortillas and bake both sheets at the same time.)

2   Cook, rotating the baking sheets halfway through baking, until golden brown and crispy, 10 to 15 minutes. Season with salt if desired immediately after taking them out of the oven, then serve.

6 to 12 corn tortillas
salt, optional

OATMEAL WITH CHARRED POBLANO PEPPERS AND CHEESE

In Mexico City, chilangos *(the local word for Mexico City residents) put charred, peeled poblano pepper strips in quesadillas or mix them with cheese and cream. I never knew anyone who put them in oatmeal, but to me, the peppers and spongy cheese crumbles add electricity to what can sometimes be a boring breakfast dish. The trick is finding a good poblano. In New York, many taste bland and washed-out, except in the summertime when local farmers' markets sometimes carry them.*

2 cups rolled oats

1 teaspoon salt

4 poblano peppers, charred, peeled and seeded (see page 37)

1 tablespoon plus 1 teaspoon olive oil

¾ cup chopped onion

4 small cloves garlic, minced

1 cup crumbled queso fresco

freshly ground black pepper, optional

crumbled cooked bacon, optional

1   In a deep microwave-safe bowl, combine the oats, ½ teaspoon salt and 3 cups water. Cook on high for 3 minutes. Stir well and cook for 3 minutes more. Alternatively, combine the same ingredients in a medium saucepan and cook over medium-high until boiling, then reduce the heat to medium-low and cook, stirring often, until all the water is absorbed and the oats are tender, about 7 minutes.

2   Cut the poblano peppers into ½-inch-wide strips. Then gather and cut into 1-inch squares. Set aside.

3   Heat the olive oil in a frying pan over medium-low heat. Add the onion and garlic and cook until aromatic, 1 minute. Stir in the poblano peppers and the remaining ½ teaspoon salt, cooking until the onions become translucent and the poblanos release a deep aroma, 4 to 5 minutes.

4   Pour the oatmeal and crumbled cheese into the pan and stir until combined. Serve in bowls, topped with freshly cracked pepper and bacon, if desired.

COOKING TIP: *Taste a small piece of the poblano before you add it to your oatmeal, just so you know how hot it is. It's also worth tasting the cheese beforehand, as sodium levels in packaged queso fresco can vary.*

NUTTY HOMEMADE MUESLI

For a long time I found muesli—a simple mix of grains, nuts and sometimes dried fruit—dry and boring compared to crunchy, snappy granola. Then I realized, muesli was much easier to make and possibly healthier. I'm a particular fan of stirring it into yogurt, which creates a thick, textured cereal as the yogurt seeps into the raw oats. This recipe includes the grains and seeds I used to see at the Mexico City licuado or milkshake and juice stands, plus walnuts, which are much easier to find in the States. The result is nutty and toasty, and packed with protein and fiber.

1   Mix the oats, seeds, amaranth, and walnuts in a medium bowl. To make one serving, mix ½ cup muesli with ½ cup yogurt and let sit for 15 minutes. Spoon over some honey or other sweetener and top with fresh or dried fruit—I like peaches, berries, cherries, raisins, or dates.

2   Store leftover muesli in an airtight container in the pantry for up to two months.

2 cups rolled oats
½ cup pumpkin seeds, toasted
2 tablespoons chia seeds
½ cup puffed amaranth (see Tip)
½ cup chopped walnuts
yogurt
honey
fresh or dried fruit

COOKING TIP: *If you can't find puffed amaranth, you can make your own from dried amaranth, which you can find at your local health food store. Heat a large heavy pot over high heat with a few grains of amaranth until those grains pop, then add 1 tablespoon of amaranth to the hot pot and shake to distribute the grains in an even layer. The amaranth will start popping immediately. Give the pot a couple more shakes until all the amaranth has popped, about 30 seconds in total, being careful not to burn it. Transfer to a bowl to cool, then return the pot to the heat and repeat until you've reached your desired yield. Four tablespoons of amaranth will yield 1 cup of puffed amaranth.*

HIBISCUS FLOWER QUESADILLAS

My friend Jesica served these quesadillas at her house several years ago, and I'd never seen anything like them. She plumped dried hibiscus flowers (weren't they only used in tea?) in water, then sautéed them in a little olive oil, butter, sugar, and chile serrano. The result, layered inside a pita pocket and slathered with cheese, was tangy and creamy, salty and slightly sweet. I've made them many times since then as a wonderful appetizer or light meal.

2½ cups hibiscus flowers
1 tablespoon unsalted butter
2 teaspoons olive oil
½ medium onion, chopped
2 serrano chiles, minced,
    with seeds
salt
1 tablespoon plus 1 teaspoon
    sugar
3 to 4 whole wheat pita pockets
8 ounces Monterey Jack cheese,
    sliced

1   Preheat the oven to 425°F. Pick over the flowers and remove any twigs or foreign matter. Rinse thoroughly in a colander under cold water.

2   Fill a medium saucepan with water and set to boil. Add the hibiscus and turn off the heat. Let sit for about 3 minutes, until fully hydrated. Drain and reserve the water for tea, if you like. Rinse the flowers under cold water to wash away any grit. Set aside.

3   Heat the butter and olive oil in a heavy-bottomed skillet over medium heat. Add the onion and chile and cook until soft, about 3 minutes. Stir in the flowers and a pinch of salt, and cook for about 2 minutes, until evenly combined.

4   Add the sugar and cook a few minutes more, stirring to coat. When the flowers have darkened to a deep-purple color, after about 3 minutes, turn off the heat.

5   Warm the pita pockets lightly in the oven or on a gently heated *comal*. Cut open the top half only, around the edge of the pitas, and tuck in a layer of cheese slices. Top with a layer of hibiscus flower filling. Place the pockets on a sheet pan in the oven until the cheese has melted, about 4 minutes. Cut into quarters and serve immediately, while the cheese is still oozy.

COOKING TIP: *In Mexico most hydrated hibiscus flowers have a chewy texture, which I like. In the States, the flowers I've found are much softer and grittier. They require a thorough rinsing both before and after you steep them, or else you get an unpleasant earthy taste in your meal. Flour tortillas can be substituted for the whole wheat pita bread, if you prefer. (For more on dried hibiscus flowers, see page 96.)*

CRISPY ZUCCHINI QUESADILLAS

I make these about once a week, using zucchini in the summer and the lighter-skinned, plumper Mexican squash the rest of the year. They're very easy to cook, and the combination of sweet squash mixed with melty cheese is unbeatable. You could really use any cooked vegetable or not-too-saucy leftovers in the fridge like spinach, mushrooms, roasted poblano peppers, roasted bell peppers, and plain shredded chicken. The key element, for me, is crisping the tortillas on the comal. *There's something about biting into a hot, crunchy quesadilla that makes it seem like you spent much more time making it than you actually did.*

2 teaspoons olive oil

3 tablespoons chopped onion

1 clove garlic, minced

1 medium zucchini, cut into
 ¼-inch-thick half-moons

salt and freshly ground black
 pepper

4 corn tortillas

3 ounces Monterrey Jack cheese,
 grated or sliced into 12 very
 thin rectangular slices

1   Heat the olive oil in a medium skillet over medium heat. Add the onion and garlic and cook until translucent, about 3 minutes. Add the zucchini and a sprinkle of salt and pepper, and cook, stirring occasionally, until the zucchini softens, about 5 minutes. Taste and adjust the seasonings.

2   Warm 2 tortillas on a *comal*, griddle or nonstick skillet over medium heat. When soft and pliable, place 3 or 4 cheese slices on one side of each tortilla. Top with an even layer of zucchini filling. Fold and press down, using the underside of a spatula if needed to hold the tortilla in place. Move the quesadillas to the outer edges of your *comal* or griddle so they don't burn.

3   If you have room, warm the remaining 2 tortillas, fill and repeat. Cook, turning occasionally, until the quesadillas are crispy on both sides and the cheese has melted, 5 to 7 minutes. Serve immediately, while the cheese is still oozy.

CREAMY KALE SALAD

I came up with this dish after craving a vaguely Mediterranean green salad that I could scoop onto a warm piece of pita bread. It ended up being sort of a salad dip—not quite one, not quite the other, and a sort of mischievous, light thing to eat for dinner when I was the only one at home. The dish works well as an appetizer, or for one person sitting alone in front of the TV. If you want less heat, use less serrano or cut out the seeds.

1 In a medium bowl, mash together the avocado, tomato, onion, chile, lime juice, and a pinch of salt, using a fork or bean masher. (The bottom of a cup also works particularly well.)

2 Press any water out of the cooked kale and chop into small pieces. If using raw kale, boil in salted water for 5 minutes or until tender. Drain well, pressing out any water. Stir into the avocado mixture and taste for more salt and lime juice. Season with pepper.

3 Top with the cilantro and pumpkin seeds.

4 Warm the pita bread on a *comal* or in a 400°F oven until hot and crisp in parts. Cut into triangles and scoop into the salad. Serve at room temperature.

1 ripe Haas avocado, peeled, pitted, and diced
¼ cup diced ripe tomato
2 tablespoons minced onion
1 small serrano chile, minced with seeds
juice of 1 lime, or more to taste
salt and freshly ground black pepper
2 cups loosely packed cooked curly kale, or 6 cups raw kale, leaves torn
1 heaping tablespoon roughly chopped fresh cilantro
2 tablespoons pumpkin seeds, toasted
2 rounds of whole wheat pita bread

CHAYOTE SALAD WITH GREEN BEANS AND TOMATOES

I ate on the street often when I lived in Mexico City, and this was the type of dish I'd cook at home when my body couldn't take any more meat or tlacoyos. Simple blanched green beans mixed with fresh tomatoes, cooked chayote, and crumbled queso fresco. It's easy and crunchy and light. Even my husband, who hates to cook, has made this salad a few times. If you can't find queso fresco, a salty, aged cheese, such as ricotta salata or feta would work, too.

8 ounces green beans, chopped
    into 2-inch pieces
salt
2 chayotes, diced into ½-inch
    pieces (about 4 cups)
3 tablespoons apple cider
    vinegar
½ teaspoon Dijon mustard
¼ teaspoon agave or honey
¼ cup olive oil
1 ripe tomato, chopped
⅔ cup chopped fresh cilantro
⅔ cup crumbled queso fresco

1   Heat a medium saucepan of water to boil. Nearby, fill a large bowl with water and ice cubes. When you've got a vigorous boil, add the green beans and a hefty dose of salt. Cook until crisp-tender and bright green, 3 to 5 minutes. Using a slotted spoon, transfer to the ice water. Let sit for about 5 minutes to stop the cooking, then drain and dry.

2   Meanwhile, place the chayote into a microwave-proof bowl and mix generously with salt. Cover with plastic wrap that's been perforated a few times with a fork. Cook until crisp-tender, 2 to 3 minutes on high. Alternatively, blanch the chayote in the same boiling water that you cooked the green beans in until crisp tender, 2 to 3 minutes, then transfer to the ice bath to stop the cooking, drain and dry.

3   Whisk together the vinegar, mustard and honey in a large bowl. Keep whisking as you add the oil in one slow stream, until fully integrated. Add the cooled chayote and green beans, and toss to coat well. Add the tomato, cilantro and cheese. Mix until combined and taste for more salt. Serve cold or at room temperature.

COOKING TIP: *Chayote, known as a "vegetable pear" in English, has a thin skin and mild flavor, and you should be able to find it at Mexican grocers or some mainstream supermarkets. The skin is so delicate that it's not worth peeling, in my opinion. Some cooks also love to eat the soft inner pit.*

HUAUZONTLE CHICKEN SOUP

Many times I've bought huauzontle at the markets because the green, fluffy stalks look so pretty. Then I've gotten home and wondered: what else can I do with this? I like eating this soup, made with just huauzontle, chicken, and rice, when I'm sick or craving something light for dinner. The nubby, fluffy huauzontle buds provide a fun contrast to the rice, and the taste is vegetal without being too overwhelming. The overall effect is healthy and soothing, and the soup freezes well, too. I usually serve this with corn tortillas I've crisped in the toaster oven.

1   Clean the huauzontle (see sidebar for detailed instructions).

2   Fill a medium saucepan two-thirds full with water, add a hefty pinch of salt and bring to a boil. Add the huauzontle and cook for 2 to 3 minutes or until just tender. Strain, discarding the cooking water.

3   Meanwhile, bring the stock to a boil in a medium pot over medium heat. Add the rice, lower the heat and simmer until barely al dente, about 12 minutes.

4   Add the huauzontle and chicken to the stock and season with salt and pepper. Cook, covered, on low heat until the rice is tender and the flavors have melded, about 5 minutes. Taste and adjust the seasonings.

5   Crisp the tortillas in an oven, sprinkling on a little salt to taste. Ladle soup into bowls and serve immediately.

1 large bunch huauzuontle
   (about 10 ounces)
salt and freshly ground black
   pepper
2 quarts Basic Homemade
   Chicken Stock (page 98)
½ cup long-grain white rice
1 cup cooked, shredded chicken
6 corn tortillas

HOW TO CLEAN HUAUZONTLES

First pluck the smaller stems from the thick center stalk of each bunch. Then take one of the small stems and, with the tips of your fingers, gently scrape off the flower buds into a bowl. (Don't do this on your nicest tablecloth, as the buds sometimes go flying everywhere.) Discard any thicker stems, which can taste bitter. Repeat until all stalks are bare. Don't be afraid of the peppery and vaguely medicinal aroma when raw; it mellows out once cooked.

STUFFED CACTUS PADDLES

These cactus paddles are loaded like potato skins, but topped with healthier ingredients: sautéed veggies, roasted peppers, a shmear of refried black beans and a sprinkle of shredded cheese. They're broiled in the oven until golden and bubbly. Depending on the size of the cactus paddles, one piece alone can make a decent meal with a side dish. Salsa also kicks things up a notch (Raw Tomatillo Salsa, page 26, goes particularly well), but it's not required.

1 batch Quick Refried Beans (page 45)

1 yellow bell pepper

6 medium cactus paddles, cleaned and de-spined (see page 146)

2 teaspoons olive oil, plus extra for coating cactus

salt and freshly ground black pepper

2 tablespoons chopped onion

1 clove garlic, minced

1 zucchini or Mexican squash, cut into thin half-moons

¾ cup grated Monterrey Jack cheese

salsa of choice

1   Make the refried beans, cover the pot and continue.

2   Roast the bell pepper over a gas flame, turning occasionally, until soft and blackened in spots. Wrap in a dish towel and let sit for 20 minutes, then peel off the skin, remove the seeds, and cut into thin strips.

3   Cut halfway into the center of each cactus paddle, making three vertical or diagonal incisions about 2 inches long. (This is for the slime to ooze out later.) Coat in olive oil and season with salt and pepper.

4   Heat a heavy skillet over medium-high heat. Working in batches, add the whole cactus paddles and cook, flipping a few times, until dark-golden brown in spots on both sides, 5 to 8 minutes per batch.

Meanwhile, heat 2 teaspoons olive oil in a medium skillet over medium heat. Add the onion and cook until translucent, 3 minutes. Stir in the garlic and cook until aromatic, 30 seconds. Then add the zucchini or squash and a light sprinkle of salt, stirring to coat. Cook, uncovered, until just tender, about 4 minutes. Stir in the bell pepper and let warm through. Taste and adjust the seasonings. This filling can be prepared up to 2 hours in advance if necessary.

5   When ready to serve, warm the refried beans and filling and set the oven to broil.

6   Place the paddles on a baking sheet. Spread with a thick layer of refried beans and top with a small mound of the filling. Finish with an even layer of grated cheese. Broil until the cheese is golden-brown and bubbly, about 3 minutes.

7   Serve immediately, passing salsa at the table.

COOKING TIP: *You can find cactus at any Mexican market. Choose firm, green paddles that don't have any brown spots.*

CACTUS FAJITAS WITH CECINA, SPINACH AND MUSHROOMS

A few years ago, while at a Tijuana restaurant with my mom, a waiter brought us a sizzling skillet of cactus, mushrooms, salty cecina steak, and rectangles of grilled panela cheese. I'd never seen anything like it in Mexico City, and I couldn't wait to try it at home. Back in New York, I added tomatoes, spinach and avocado, and swapped out the panela for Dominican queso de freír, a mild, not-too-salty cheese that doesn't melt when fried (and is much easier for me to find in my neighborhood). The tumble of vegetables and smoky meat feels sort of Tex-Mex, which is why I call them fajitas.

1   Heat a large cast-iron skillet over medium-high heat. Working in batches, add the steak in a single layer and cook for about 2 minutes per side, until dark-golden brown and the meat starts to release clear juices. Transfer to a plate and let cool. Slice into ½-inch by 2-inch strips.

2   Cut the cactus paddles into ½-inch by 2-inch strips. Place in medium bowl and season with salt and pepper. Toss with about 1 tablespoon of the olive oil to coat.

3   Heat a large skillet over medium-high heat. Working in batches, add the cactus in a single layer and cook, undisturbed, for about 2 minutes until it begins to brown. Then cook, uncovered, stirring occasionally, until golden brown on both sides and tender, about 6 minutes. Transfer to a bowl and set aside.

4   In the same pan, heat the remaining 1 tablespoon olive oil over high heat. Add the mushrooms and cook until tender and browned, about 5 minutes. Toss in the spinach, tomatoes and salt to taste. Turn up the heat if necessary to evaporate some of the juices.

5   Meanwhile, heat the canola oil in a medium nonstick frying pan over medium heat. Add the cheese slices in an even layer. Cook, turning once, until a dark-golden crust develops on both sides, 4 to 6 minutes. Transfer to a plate.

6   Add the cactus and steak to the vegetables, and stir to combine. Taste for more salt and cook until warmed through. Transfer to a platter, draining off some of the juice if necessary. Top with the fried cheese and cilantro.

7   Heat the tortillas on a *comal* or nonstick skillet until soft and pliable, and place in a cloth or basket to keep warm. Serve the platter at the table, passing the basket of tortillas, avocado slices, lime wedges and salsa for guests to make their own tacos.

1 pound *cecina* steak (see page 80), cut into large pieces

1 pound cactus paddles, de-spined and rinsed (see page 146)

salt and freshly ground black pepper

2 tablespoons olive oil

1 (8-ounce) package crimini or baby bella mushrooms, sliced ¼ inch thick

1 large bunch spinach, washed and spun dry

1 large tomato, cut into chunks

1 tablespoon canola oil

8 ounces panela cheese or Dominican queso de freír, cut into rectangles

¼ cup roughly chopped fresh cilantro

20 corn tortillas

1 to 2 ripe Haas avocados, peeled, pitted and sliced

5 limes, cut into wedges

salsa of choice

COOKING TIP: *You can find panela cheese in Mexican grocery stores in cities with large Hispanic populations. Queso de freír is generally sold in square blocks at Caribbean markets (I like the Tropical brand).*

CURRIED CAULIFLOWER TACOS WITH ROASTED TOMATILLO CHUTNEY

One thing I learned in Mexico is that you can taco anything. (There's actually a verb for it, taquear.*) Taco-ing not only stretches the meal—tortillas require smaller portions—but foods just seem more complete when wrapped in a tortilla, even if you're only serving one ingredient.*

I visited India while I was living in Mexico, and when I got back, I made tacos from all sorts of curries. (One of my friends teased me about opening an "Indo-Mex" food truck someday.) This one, made with roasted, browned cauliflower, makes a lot of sense in New York, where the variety of fresh vegetables drops severely in the winter. The chutney-salsa hybrid mixes tomatillos with grated coconut—creamy, sweet, and acidic—and is mandatory with this dish.

1 teaspoon mustard seeds
2½ teaspoons spicy curry powder
1¼ teaspoons salt
½ cup olive oil
1 large head cauliflower or two small, chopped into florets
2 medium onions, quartered
12 corn tortillas

For the chutney:
5 small tomatillos, husked and rinsed
1 serrano chile
3 tablespoons grated fresh coconut, or ¼ cup unsweetened dried coconut flakes
1 teaspoon canola oil
½ teaspoon mustard seeds
1 teaspoon *urad dal* or raw unsalted peanuts
4 fresh curry leaves
salt

1   Preheat the oven to 450°F. In a large bowl, mix the mustard seeds, curry powder and salt until well combined. Add the olive oil in a slow pour, whisking everything together. Taste and adjust the salt.

2   Add the cauliflower and onion, breaking apart the onion pieces with your fingers and mixing everything together thoroughly with your hands, until the vegetables are evenly coated. Transfer to a baking sheet and roast until dark-golden brown and crispy in spots, 30 to 40 minutes.

3   Meanwhile, prepare the chutney: Roast the tomatillos and chile on a *comal* or nonstick skillet until blackened in spots. Transfer to a bowl to cool, then chop into smaller pieces. Place in a blender jar with the coconut and blend until smooth, adding a little water if necessary to help the blades turn. Transfer to a small bowl.

4   Heat the canola oil in a small skillet over medium-high heat. Add the mustard seeds and *urad dal*. When the seeds begin popping, immediately remove the pan from the heat and add the curry leaves. Pour into the chutney and mix well. Season with salt.

5   Warm the tortillas on a *comal* or nonstick skillet and place in a cloth or basket to keep warm. Transfer the curried cauliflower to a serving bowl, and pass the tortillas and chutney at the table, so each guest can make their own tacos.

COOKING TIP: *You can find mustard seeds, fresh curry leaves and* urad dal*—a type of nutty lentil—at Indian grocers, or you can substitute peanuts for the* urad dal. *Don't leave out the fresh curry leaves if you can help it, and use the smallest tomatillos you can find—they'll blacken more easily on the* comal.

FISH TACOS WITH CREAMY PASILLA OAXACA SAUCE

I can never decide which type of fish tacos I like better: battered and fried, for the crunch and texture, or pan-fried because they're healthier and only need a few minutes to make? So I'm giving you both versions here, both topped with a pile of fresh cabbage and a creamy, hot salsa. The latter is my favorite part of the dish, made from the smoky Oaxacan pasilla chile, not the pasilla generally sold in Mexican markets. You want the one that is berry-colored, wrinkly and extremely hot, easily found online—and you'll want to stockpile them in your pantry, because they're that good.

1 To make the battered fish, in a medium bowl, whisk together the flour and 1 teaspoon salt. Pour in the beer, whisking until a thick batter forms; it will be lumpy. Set aside in the fridge.

2 Heat the oil in a deep pot to 350°F. Place about ¼ cup flour on a plate, and season the fish on both sides with salt and pepper.

3 When the oil is ready, dredge the fish pieces lightly in flour and shake off any excess. Dunk the fish pieces in the beer batter one at a time, and place in the hot oil. Fry for about 3 minutes per side until golden. Drain on paper towels.

4 To make the pan-fried fish, rinse and pat the fish dry. Season with salt and pepper. Pour the oil in a nonstick skillet and heat to medium. Add the fish and cook until the flesh is juicy and flaky, and the fish is golden-brown, about 3 minutes per side.

5 To serve, warm the corn tortillas on a *comal* or nonstick skillet. Place one piece of battered fish, or a generous helping of pan-fried fish, in a tortilla and drizzle with lime juice. Top with chile pasilla cream sauce and thinly sliced cabbage. Serve immediately, passing additional sauce at the table.

COOKING TIP: *I've made these tacos with trout, hake and pollock, and all have worked well. If you can't find Oaxacan pasilla chile, substitute chile morita. Also, if you don't like very spicy salsas, double the amount of yogurt and mayo.*

For battered and fried fish tacos:
1 cup flour, plus extra for dredging
salt and freshly ground black pepper
1¼ cup light beer, preferably Modelo Especial
canola oil
1 pound fish fillets, cut into 2- to 3-inch fingers

For pan-fried fish tacos:
1 pound fish fillets, sliced into 4 pieces
salt and freshly ground black pepper
1 tablespoon olive oil

12 corn tortillas
3 limes, sliced into wedges
Chile Pasilla Cream Sauce (recipe follows)
2 cups thinly sliced cabbage

CHILE PASILLA CREAM SAUCE

1 Make an incision in the chile and scrape out the seeds and veins with a small spoon or butter knife. (Don't use your fingers, as the chile is very hot.) Cover the chile in hot water and let hydrate until the skin has softened, about 20 minutes.

2 Add the chile, garlic, yogurt, and mayonnaise to a blender jar with 1 to 2 tablespoons water. (Using chile water in this instance would make the sauce extremely spicy—if you do it, proceed with caution.) Blend until as smooth as possible. Taste for salt and add if necessary. Refrigerate until ready to use.

1 Oaxaca chile pasilla
1 clove garlic, minced
2 tablespoons plain yogurt (not Greek)
1 tablespoon mayonnaise
salt

PASTA WITH ANCHO CHILES, MUSHROOMS AND GARLIC

This recipe is a twist on champiñones al ajillo, *the Spanish dish of garlicky, slightly spicy mushrooms. The anchos here almost act as a vegetable, lending a hint of sweetness and creaminess. A lot of garlic is necessary: it infuses the olive oil at the start of the dish, which then coats the mushrooms and the chiles. I like topping this with a slightly aged cheese (Parmesan or Mexican queso añejo) and chopped, lightly briny black olives, which brings out the bitter notes in the chiles. If you don't eat gluten, this also works excellently as a taco filling without the pasta.*

3 large ancho chiles

11 cloves garlic

8 ounces dried fettuccine noodles

¼ cup olive oil, plus extra if needed

1 large bunch (about 13½ ounces) oyster mushrooms, torn into very thin strips

salt

½ cup chopped, lightly briny black olives, for garnish

½ cup grated queso añejo or Parmesan, for garnish

1   Snip the stems off the anchos and cut an incision in each. Scrape out the seeds and veins with a spoon or knife. Place the chiles in a bowl and cover with warm water. Let sit for about 20 minutes, until the flesh has softened.

2   Meanwhile, peel the garlic cloves and slice thinly.

3   Bring a pot of water to boil. Add the pasta and cook until al dente, 10 to 12 minutes. Drain and set aside, reserving ½ cup of the pasta water.

4   Cut the softened chiles into ½-inch strips—I do this by rolling them up like a burrito first, and then chopping width-wise.

5   Heat the oil in a heavy-bottomed skillet over medium-high heat. Add the garlic and cook until slightly browned, about 2 minutes. Add the chiles and stir quickly, making sure the garlic doesn't burn. Lower the heat if you need to.

6   Once the chiles have become aromatic, stir in the mushrooms and cook until softened, 5 to 10 minutes, adding salt once the mushrooms have released their juices.

7   Add the pasta to your mushroom mixture, with a little of the reserved pasta water and extra oil to make it more saucy if you like. Serve immediately in shallow bowls, topped with chopped olives and a dusting of cheese.

COOKING TIPS: *I chose oyster mushrooms because they're abundant in Mexico and because I like their chewy texture. If you can't find them, substitute shiitake or crimini. Also, if you can find already peeled garlic cloves, use them—peeling is the step that takes the most time.*

Look for soft, pliable dried chiles. Brittle chiles won't rehydrate well and the flesh won't break down while cooking. You can also soften them on a comal beforehand in order to remove the seeds.

SOPA WITH SPINACH AND CHEESE

We ate my mom's sopa at least once a month growing up, which was sort of like Fideo Noodles in Chipotle-Tomato Sauce (page 102), except less complicated. It calls for canned tomato sauce, a little onion, and salt. I dress mine up to my own tastes by adding sautéed spinach or chard, and some crumbled cheese. The pasta is still fried in oil beforehand, and because they're shells, little bits of sauce cling to their insides. In Mexico, sopa seca is a side dish. In my house, we've always eaten it as a main meal.

2 teaspoons canola oil, plus more for cooking greens

4 thin slices onion

1 (7-ounce) package small pasta shells

1 (8-ounce) can tomato sauce

salt

6 to 8 cups spinach leaves, rinsed and dried

1 hunk queso fresco, or any other farmer's style white cheese, crumbled

1   Heat the oil in a medium saucepan over medium-high heat. When hot, add the onion and pasta shells and cook, stirring constantly, for 5 to 8 minutes until the pasta is toasty, and the edges turn a deep golden brown. (It's okay if the onion burns a little.)

2   Add the tomato sauce and 3 cups water in one quick pour. (The pot may hiss and splatter.) Season with salt, cover, and lower the heat. Simmer gently for about 12 minutes, until the pasta shells are al dente and have soaked up the sauce. If you're unsure, take off the lid and peek in on it once in a while. It won't hurt the dish.

3   Heat a small amount of oil in a large skillet over medium heat. Add the spinach and sauté until wilted but still a deep green color. Season with salt. Scrape the spinach into four separate bowls, and top with a few scoops of *sopa* and cheese. Serve warm.

COOKING TIP: *Canned tomato sauce is not spaghetti sauce. It's just puréed tomato and salt, generally sold in small cans in the soup aisle of any American grocery store. Small pasta shells can be found in Mexican markets, usually next to fideo noodles. You can use any other pasta or noodle you like.*

AMARANTH AND PUMPKIN SEED-CRUSTED CHICKEN WITH CREAMY POMEGRANATE DIPPING SAUCE

Some days I don't crave any acidity or heat at all. (Can you believe it, after reading this book?) On those days, I eat something simple like roast chicken and vegetables, or these baked chicken cutlets, coated in a crunchy, mild mix of puffed amaranth, pumpkin seeds and panko bread crumbs. They're like a more elegant chicken finger, served with a fun (purple-colored!), slightly sweet, slightly smoky dipping sauce. This dish is easy to throw together, and if you know you'll be pressed for time, you could mix the dry ingredients a day or two beforehand. Salad or roasted or steamed vegetables work just fine as a side.

1   First make the creamy pomegranate sauce: Pour the pomegranate juice into a small saucepan over medium-high heat and reduce for 15 minutes; you should end up with about ¼ cup syrup. Transfer to a bowl and let cool. Stir in the rest of the sauce ingredients and set aside.

2   Preheat the oven to 350°F. In a medium bowl, mix together the panko crumbs, puffed amaranth, pumpkin seeds, ¾ teaspoon salt, ¼ teaspoon pepper, thyme and oregano.

3   Season the chicken cutlets with salt.

4   Pour the flour onto a plate, and place the beaten egg and the amaranth mixture nearby in two shallow bowls. Grease a baking sheet lightly with olive oil.

5   Dredge one chicken cutlet in the flour, shaking off any excess. Dip in the egg, then press into the amaranth and pumpkin seed mixture, covering the cutlet evenly.

6   Place the cutlet on the baking sheet and repeat with the remaining cutlets. Bake for 20 minutes, or until the chicken is juicy and no longer pink. For a crispier crust, finish under the broiler for 2 minutes.

7   Serve with room-temperature creamy pomegranate sauce.

For the creamy pomegranate sauce:

1 cup unsweetened pomegranate juice, such as POM brand
¼ cup sour cream
⅛ scant teaspoon smoked paprika (not sweet)
freshly ground black pepper

½ cup panko crumbs
1 cup puffed amaranth (see Tip)
½ cup pumpkin seeds
salt and freshly ground black pepper
1½ teaspoons fresh thyme
1 teaspoon dried Mexican oregano
1½ pounds chicken cutlets
⅓ cup flour
2 eggs, lightly beaten
olive oil

COOKING TIP: *You should be able to find amaranth—a native Mexican grain—at health food stores or online. If you can't find puffed amaranth, you can make your own from dried amaranth (see page 163).*

CABBAGE ENCHILADAS

*I remember the day when my husband came home from work and asked, "What's for dinner?"
I said, "Cabbage enchiladas!" And he grimaced. Yet after a few bites, he was a convert. Cooked
cabbage, naturally sweet, pairs well with spicy enchilada sauce, and the dish is spunkier than the
usual cabbage offerings of coleslaw, salads, and corned beef. These are inspired by enchiladas
queretanas, a dark-red enchilada native to the state of Querétaro. They're traditionally served
topped with fried potatoes, lightly pickled jalapeños and carrots.*

1   Fill a medium saucepan two-thirds full with water and bring to a boil. Add the
potatoes and cook until just tender when pricked with a fork, about 20 minutes. Drain
and set aside to cool, then cut into small dice.

2   Meanwhile, heat a *comal* or nonstick skillet to medium-low heat. Toast the chiles
lightly, turning frequently, until they release a spicy aroma, about 20 seconds. Place the
garlic cloves near the edge of the pan and roast until soft and squishy, 5 to 10 minutes.
Transfer the chiles to a clean workspace, snip off the stems and remove the seeds. Place
the chiles in a bowl of warm water and let sit for about 20 minutes, until the skins
soften. Peel the garlic and set aside.

3   While the chiles soak, warm 2 teaspoons oil in a large skillet over medium heat.
Add the onion and cook until translucent, about 3 minutes. Add the minced garlic and
cook until aromatic, about 30 seconds. Add the cabbage and ½ cup water and bring to
a boil. Season with salt, reduce heat to low and simmer, covered, until the cabbage is
soft and tender, about 10 minutes. Taste and adjust salt. Keep warm, covered.

4   In a medium frying pan, heat 1 tablespoon oil to medium heat and add the potatoes.
Season with salt and cook, undisturbed, for about 4 minutes, or until a golden-brown
crust forms on the bottom. Flip and cook the other side, seasoning lightly with salt.
Once both sides are crisp, lower the heat, cover, and cook until the potatoes are crunchy
on the outside but soft in the middle, 12 to 15 minutes. Keep warm.

5   Place the chiles, garlic, and 1½ cups water in a blender jar, and blend until smooth
but fairly thick, not thin and soupy. Heat 1 teaspoon lard in a medium saucepan. When
hot, add the sauce in one quick pour, stirring. (Careful, it may splatter.) Season with
¾ teaspoon salt and cook until the flavors meld, about 5 minutes. Keep warm.

6   In a small frying pan, heat 2 teaspoons oil over medium heat. Add one tortilla
and cook, flipping once, until slightly tougher but not crisp, 20 to 25 seconds. Using
tongs, quickly dip in the warm enchilada sauce, making sure the sauce coats both
sides. Transfer to a plate and add a generous amount of cabbage. Roll into a tube, then
repeat with another tortilla. Top the enchiladas with fried potatoes, pickled jalapeño,
queso fresco, and chopped cilantro. Serve immediately, and then repeat with the
remaining enchiladas.

2 large, waxy potatoes
5 guajillo chiles
4 ancho chiles
2 cloves garlic, unpeeled, plus
   1 clove, minced
4 teaspoons plus 1 tablespoon
   canola oil, plus more for frying
1 small onion, chopped
1 small head cabbage, sliced into
   very thin shreds
salt
1 teaspoon lard or canola oil
8 corn tortillas
1 small can pickled jalapeño
   strips
1 cup crumbled queso fresco
½ to ¾ cup chopped fresh
   cilantro

COOKING TIP: *Enchiladas
should be served immediately, which
means the cook is often stuck in the
kitchen while everyone else is eating.
For that reason, it's helpful to have
a friend (or significant other) in the
kitchen helping stuff and assemble,
if possible.*

TOMATO MILPA PIE

I hadn't heard of tomato pie until I married my husband, whose family is from South Carolina. It's a typical Southern dish of fresh tomatoes sliced and layered in a cooked piecrust. The tomatoes are blanketed with cheese and mayonnaise, then baked. To help round the dish out, I like throwing in squash and corn, two items traditionally found in the Mexican farming plot known as a milpa, an ancient multi-crop farming system, in which three items—beans, squash and corn—are farmed together to work synergistically. I don't use beans in this recipe, but a sprinkle of cooked black or pinto beans might be fun, now that I think about it.

For the piecrust:
1¼ cups all-purpose flour
½ teaspoon salt
½ teaspoon sugar
½ cup (1 stick) cold unsalted
    butter

For the filling:
2 pounds fresh, ripe tomatoes
salt
2 tablespoons olive oil
½ medium onion, chopped
1 garlic clove, minced
1 small Mexican squash or
    zucchini, cut into thin
    half-moons
1 heaping cup fresh corn kernels
salt
⅓ cup mayonnaise
1 cup shredded Monterrey Jack
    cheese, or a mix of Monterrey
    Jack and Swiss
¼ cup chopped fresh cilantro

COOKING TIPS: *This recipe traditionally calls for much more mayonnaise, but I've cut back to save a few calories. This means the topping is more mottled than smooth. It's still delicious.*

Any cheese would work here— mozzarella, Gruyère, Swiss. Or mix them up.

1 Fill a small bowl with ½ cup water and add a few ice cubes.

2 In a medium bowl, whisk together the flour, salt and sugar. Using a pastry blender, or two knives, cut in the butter until it breaks into uneven, more-or-less pea-shaped pieces. Add 1 tablespoon ice water at a time to the mixture, until the dough just comes together when squeezed. Shape the dough into a ball and wrap in plastic wrap. Flatten into a disk and refrigerate for at least 1 hour. (You can freeze the dough for less time if you're in a hurry, but if you overfreeze, the dough will be impossible to roll out.)

3 Place the dough on a well-floured workspace. With a floured rolling pin, roll the dough into an 11-inch circle, gently peeling the dough off the workspace and rotating in a circle as needed. Transfer the dough to a 9-inch pie plate and trim off any excess. Pinch or crimp the ends. If the crust has softened too much and feels greasy, place it in the refrigerator to chill for about 30 minutes. Meanwhile, preheat the oven to 400°F.

4 Cover the piecrust with a layer of foil (this will prevent it from browning too soon in the oven), and weigh it down with a layer of dried beans. Bake for 20 minutes, then remove the foil and bake for 5 to 10 minutes more, until the crust is golden brown. Let cool while you make the filling, and lower the oven to 350°F.

5 Slice the tomatoes into ¼-inch slices and sprinkle with salt (you can blanch and peel them, first, if you're picky about skins). Place in a colander and let sit for at least 20 minutes to help the tomatoes release their juices, which will make the pie less soggy.

6 Heat the oil in a medium skillet over medium heat. Add the onion and cook until translucent, 4 to 5 minutes. Add the garlic and cook until aromatic, about 30 seconds. Stir in the squash and corn and cook until the squash is just tender, 6 to 7 minutes. Season with salt and set aside.

7 Pat the tomatoes dry with paper towels. Mix together the mayonnaise and cheese in a small bowl. Place half of the tomatoes in an even layer in the cooled piecrust. Top with half of the squash mixture, and a sprinkle of cilantro. Repeat layers with remaining tomatoes and squash, then slather the mayonnaise-cheese mixture evenly over the top.

8 Bake for about 25 minutes or until lightly browned. Let the pie cool slightly, then serve warm. The pie is best the day it's made—it will become soggy in the fridge.

DARK CHOCOLATE CHICHARRÓN COOKIES

I love anything sweet and savory, so this snack makes perfect sense to me: chicharrón—*fluffy, salty, fried pork skin—is mixed with dark chocolate in a buttery, dense cookie. It's not too far removed from chocolate and bacon (another fabulous combination), but with a heartier crunch. My sense is that most* chilangos *would be weirded out by this pairing, because in Mexico City,* chicharrón *is always used in a savory context.*

You can find chicharrón *at most Mexican markets, and they may offer a couple varieties: thinner, lighter sheets, and thicker sheets curled at the edges, speckled with bits of meat. For the purposes of this cookie, it's best to use the lighter, meatless variety. (The meatier stuff is great with salsa, though.) If you can't find it, packaged* chicharrón *works—I like the Baken-ets variety, which is available at most grocery stores.*

1 Whisk together the flour, baking soda, and salt in a medium bowl. Set aside.

2 In the bowl of a standing mixer, beat together the eggs and both sugars until light and fluffy and doubled in volume, about 3 minutes. Lower the speed, and mix in the butter and vanilla until well combined.

3 Using a wooden spoon or rubber spatula, stir the dry mixture into the wet until just combined. Gently stir in the chocolate and *chicharrón*, being careful not to over-mix.

4 Cover the dough with plastic wrap and let sit in the refrigerator until firm, at least 2 hours, or ideally overnight.

5 When ready to bake, preheat the oven to 350°F. Drop the cookies by mounded tablespoonfuls onto an ungreased baking sheet, spacing them about 2 inches apart. Cook for 10 to 12 minutes, or until the edges just start to brown and the middles are still soft.

6 Let cool on the baking sheet for 1 minute, then remove to a wire rack to cool completely.

2¼ cups all-purpose flour

1 teaspoon baking soda

1 teaspoon salt

2 large eggs

¾ cup sugar

¾ cup packed light brown sugar

½ cup (2 sticks) unsalted butter, melted and cooled to room temperature

1 teaspoon vanilla extract

7 ounces dark chocolate (at least 70% cacao), chopped into ¼-inch chunks

1 cup crumbled *chicharrón* (pork cracklings)

COOKING TIPS: *To crumble the* chicharrón, *if it's very hard, place it in a plastic bag and whack it with a meat pounder or a frying pan.*

The cookies taste best if you chill the dough overnight in the fridge—resting time allows the dough to develop more flavor. They'll keep for 4 days in an airtight container.

ACKNOWLEDGMENTS

So many people helped make this cookbook a reality. My editor, Anja Schmidt, believed in the idea from the beginning, and I'm grateful to her and the team at Kyle Books. Thanks to Blair Richardson for her hard work on the design and to my agent Jeff Ourvan for his guidance and support. My cooking assistant and friend, Girelle Guzmán, kept me motivated, as did recipe testers Mira Evnine and Anna Stockwell, my brother Chris Téllez (who prepared the dishes with gusto for his three children) and Josh Keller. Jesica López Sol shared her enthusiasm for Mexican cuisine with me early on, and let me know it was okay to share this culture even if I didn't grow up in it.

Special thanks to Mexico City food vendors and friends who lent me their recipes, walked me through a technique, or directly inspired a dish: Erick Valle, Luís Buenrostro Guitérrez, Victor Hugo Quiróz Pérez, Amparo Reina Rendón, Jorge León, Juan Carlos Martínez, Angélica Nápoles, Abel Rodriguez and Emma Villanueva Buendía, Miguel Garduño and his mother Sra. Paty, Janneth López, Nick Zukin, Alonso Ruvalcaba, Graciela Montaño and the staff at Burrería a Todo Mecate, Con Sabor a Tixtla and Tacos Don Guero, Sra. Rosa Peña Sotres and her daughter Delia, and Sra. Margarita of the *tortillería* on Calle Aranda. *Gracias* to Arturo Anzaldo for doing the legwork when I couldn't be in DF, and to my team at Eat Mexico Culinary Tours for holding down the fort while I slogged away writing recipes. I'm grateful, too, to Marcela Landres, Katherine Fausset and Penny De Los Santos, who listened to my ideas about this book several years ago and encouraged me to pursue it. I'm immensely grateful to Liz and Erik Vance for giving me a home in DF.

Thank you to the Escuela de Gastronomía Mexicana for teaching me about the cuisine of my *antepasados*. To my parents, who taught me to be curious and take pleasure in food, I owe you homemade tortillas every day for the rest of my life. And finally, thanks to Crayton, whose early morning trips to the *tortillería*, grocery buying, and all-around cheerleading made this project possible.